Keep On Pushing
Hot Lessons From Cool Runnings

ISBN: 978-0-9764082-7-7

Library of Congress Control Number: 2009939365

Keep On Pushing: Hot Lessons From Cool Runnings/Devon Harris

1. Devon Harris, 1964-
2. Olympic Games—Jamaica—Biography
3. Bobsledding—Jamaica—Biography
4. Inspirational

Printed in Hong Kong
www.devonharris.com

THIS BOOK IS LOVINGLY DEDICATED TO:

My wife, Nicole.
Thanks for your love and unwavering support

The memory of my grandmother, Loretta Robinson.
You fired up my imagination and turned me into a dreamer.

Acknowledgments

Oh Lord, when I think of where I am coming from and where I am today, I have to say thank you!

Writing a book is an enormous undertaking that requires the help of others to get it done.

The books I have read and the tapes and speeches I have listened to over the years have provided me with invaluable insights as I crafted this book. The many conversations that I have had with friends have also been precious. Thanks guys for jogging my memory with your stimulating discourse.

Special thanks to Stephen Samuels for reading the manuscript multiple times and giving his honest opinion during those long, spirited conversations we had.

Steve Hochman, my brother from another mother, your candor was very helpful as well.

Table of Contents

Table of Contents (cont.)

Introduction

I t is 1993, and I am walking briskly up Gun Hill Road in the Bronx, the frigid pre-dawn wind sweeping across my face. I remember this winter date – January 18th – very clearly. It was Martin Luther King, Jr. Day, and I was on my way to my first day of work at the Jamaican restaurant just up the road.

I arrived in the United States just three weeks prior, on December 23rd. Two days later, on Christmas Day, I celebrated my 28th birthday in my new home, my new country. When I boarded the flight in Kingston, I was still officially a captain in the Jamaica Defence Force (JDF). Back then, the only time I went into a kitchen was to inspect it. Now I was on my way to start working in one as a line cook. Less than a year before I was in Albertville, France competing in my second Olympic Games. And now, as tens of millions before me had done, I had come to America to chase my American dream.

So here I am on a day that honors the quintessential American dreamer, inhaling the wintry air and wondering what life in America had in store for me. Decades before, Dr. King had clearly defined *his* dream, and although I still wasn't clear about what *mine* looked like, I had high hopes. I slackened my pace momentarily, closed my eyes and inhaled deeply. As the cold air filled my lungs, I could feel the possibilities permeating every fiber of my being. But my most pressing need that day was to begin that new job, and I was grateful for the work as I had a wife and a two-year-old son to support.

Flash forward sixteen years. I still find myself spending a lot of time in the kitchen, only this time I am preparing meals for my family in my home just north of New York City. If – or more accurately – when, my wife, Nicole, a respiratory therapist, gets her way, I will be living on the water in a warmer part of the United States. Unlike her, I like my water frozen, and I would choose cold weather over the tropical heat any day. She scratches her head every time I say that. "Where were you born?" she would ask mockingly. But I love it here. The changing seasons remind me of the rhythms of my life. My favorite is autumn; I am enthralled by the beauty of brown, yellow and orange leaves breaking up the city skyline through the branches and then finally falling and carpeting the ground.

I am writing this introduction on my laptop, sitting in my backyard, and trying to convince my fourth of five children, Summer, to play on her slide. For now, she is much more interested in playing one of her games on my computer. I know that three-year-olds can be very persistent, but she seems to be even more so than most. I wonder where she could have gotten *that* from?

As the scent of freshly mowed grass permeates the air, I know the sputter I hear in the distance is my neighbor's lawn mower, and not the gunshots that used to be my lullaby as I would fall off to sleep in our Kingston home.

The oldest of fifteen brothers and sisters, I grew up with half of my siblings. Like everyone else around us, we managed to find peace and security in the middle of the chaos and danger that enveloped us. I look back now and realize how terrified we really were.

Every single day I am reminded of how far I have traveled. From the slums of Olympic Gardens, living in a two-room wooden shack, to the prestige of the Royal Military Academy Sandhurst and the officer corps of the Jamaica Defence Force, where I smoothed out my rough ghetto edges and learned to be a gentleman. From dreaming about running track in the Olympics, to competing in three Olympics as a member of Jamaica's historic bobsled team. From being shot at on the streets of Kingston, to being on a feature film set watching a Hollywood movie being shot about an important part of my life.

Today, I travel around the world as a motivational speaker, giving keynote addresses and workshops to audiences full of senior executives from Fortune 100 corporations, sharing a lifetime of lessons learned about perseverance and teamwork. My foundation creates and runs programs aimed at improving the lives of less fortunate children across the globe. As often as I can, I visit schools and speak to the children. I encourage *them* to always have a dream, and to work hard towards making that dream come true.

I still marvel at the fact that, as small as Jamaica is, as a kid I didn't even know where the airport was. Now, I make my way through airports around the globe with the ease and familiarity of a seasoned traveler. To think that the greatest businesses around the world find value in what a barefoot boy from a Kingston ghetto has to say, or that I may be able to inspire a poor child who has some big dreams of her own, is humbling, exhilarating, gratifying. It is a huge responsibility and I take it seriously.

In some ways this sounds like the stuff that Hollywood movies are made of. And, of course, after *Cool Runnings'* great success, it is literally true.

I am so grateful to God. All this used to be a dream. Now I am living it. I live it every day. Yeah mon, I love it!

Even as I encourage *them* to **Keep On Pushing**, I keep pushing *myself* as well. Pointing to the *great* things I have done in the past is wonderful, but the real power of my message lies in what I am doing with my life today. We all must find a way to **Keep On Pushing**.

During the eighteen months I worked in that restaurant on Gun Hill Road, there were many times I was tempted to settle for what I had in hand. I rationalized that if I lived frugally, if I scrimped and saved, I could carve out a fairly decent life in the Bronx. I was tempted to give up on dreaming big dreams, to become complacent and blend in with the crowd, to settle for far less than what I knew was possible. I came close a few times to doing just that, but there was a voice inside of me that pushed me to do the opposite. It is the same voice that is inside of you. If you listen carefully, you will hear it telling you, "You are more than this." "There is greatness inside of you." "There is much more that you can do." I chose to listen to that voice. I kept on pushing, and now I have the opportunity to travel the world and inspire audiences with my story. I believe it is our responsibility to **Keep On Pushing**, to grow as individuals and to strive towards our full potential.

In 1979, the year I started running track, ABC's *Wide World of Sports* ran a series called "Road to Moscow." The series took a peek into the lives of Olympic hopefuls from around the world who were working to compete in the 1980 Summer Games in Moscow. It not only highlighted their athletic lives, but also their personal lives. What I took away from the series was that Olympic athletes were average and ordinary people with extraordinary dreams and an equally strong desire and drive to achieve them. It occurred to me, then, that virtually anyone can attain high levels of achievement if they are willing to push themselves long and hard enough.

If you have ever wondered about what it takes to qualify for the Olympics, or asked yourself what it must be like to live in the Olympic Village, or how it felt to be front and center in the competition arena; if you are one of the people who believe that bobsleds run on rails, bobsledders are nuts, or that the movie *Cool Runnings* is a purely fictionalized story, then **Keep On Pushing: Hot Lessons from Cool Runnings** is for you.

This book is your front row seat to the life of an Olympic athlete, and your ticket to the world of Olympic bobsledding.

These pages will tell you of the hardships and difficulties Olympic athletes face in qualifying for the Games, and the sense of achievement they feel when they finally march in the Opening Ceremonies.

The ensuing chapters will transport you to the real world of bobsledding – its rigors, dangers, excitement and exhilaration. You will learn about the passion that drives them to compete so fiercely, and how that same passion can drive you to achieve your goals.

I wrote **Keep On Pushing** to engage you in a conversation about how you can always push yourself past the obstacles in your life to higher levels of achievement. I wrote it to inspire you and to give you tools that worked for me as well as my corporate clients, tools that you can immediately apply to your life.

In keeping with my desire to both encourage and challenge, and my wish to see you apply the lessons that I am passing on to you in this book, you will find a section at the end of each chapter entitled "Key Points to Remember." These are the most salient points in the chapter. Review them frequently. They will serve as your own motivational booster to get you through the day. In time, you will find that they have significantly influenced your thinking as you embrace this philosophy of **Keep On Pushing.**

You will also find an assignment at the end of each chapter. Put time aside to do them. My suggestion is that you read through the book once and then, as you go through it again perhaps more slowly, spend some time digesting the Key Points to Remember before completing each assignment and moving to the next chapter.

You will notice that I have included quotes from several well-known persons, as well as some whom you may not easily recognize. That's because I believe that everyone who has succeeded, whether they are famous or less well-known, can contribute to our growth and development. As a result, I have taken inspiration from all of them. I hope you will too.

You will read about how I made up my own training programs in high school after reading books on middle distance running. I encourage you to do the same here. No one knows you and your heart's desire the way you do. It is your life. Shape it in the way you want. This book is a tool to help you dream, plan, and execute... so use it!

And, as always: Keep On Pushing!

Devon Harris

Keep On Pushing

"Man was created as a being who should constantly keep improving, a being who on reaching one goal sets a higher one."

Ralph Ransom - American Writer

I n bobsledding, the uninformed observer only sees, at the start, the massive pushing of the sled from the starting blocks. However, anyone who has learned how to push a bobsled knows that there are different phases of the push, each designed to apply constant pressure on the sled while exerting maximum effort and ultimately attaining the best result. First, there is the explosive force of the push on the sled as the team pushers overcome inertia to get the 650-lb. mass of fiberglass and metal moving. Should they stop there, the sled would eventually come to a stop or slowly trickle along the slippery ice until gravity starts pulling it down the track. From there, they transition into their running form, plowing through the first fifteen meters of the ice, constantly applying pressure to the sled and accelerating down the hill.

The common mistake that most beginner brakemen make is to take their hands off the push bar as they transition from their initial burst of force on the sled to a normal running form. The secret is to rotate your hands as you change grips. If you take your hands off the push bar you run the risk of falling. As the sled comes out of the blocks, the brakeman's body is at about a thirty degree angle. This position leaves him slightly off balance. With the piston-like movement of his feet keeping him ahead of the sled, his hands on the push bar keep him balanced until he is able to get into a normal running form. The other important reason to always keep your hands on the push bar is that if you remove them, even for a split second, you are not pushing, and are therefore wasting valuable time.

When the sled is going as fast as the pusher is running he is in effect no longer pushing. At that point he jumps in, using his momentum and the weight of his body to give the sled one final jolt forward. Because the start is such a critical part of the race, it is important that the athlete keeps pushing the sled until it has developed enough momentum to travel under its own power. Once the sled is traveling under its own power, applying the brakes will slow it down; but its momentum and the pull of gravity means that it is virtually impossible to stop it.

The same holds true for us in life. Every desire, every worthwhile goal, every dream that you have in life is sitting on its equivalent of a 650-lb. bobsled. In order to make them a reality, you must launch with maximum effort and then continue to push forward with zest. As with the bobsled athlete, when you begin to make steady progress towards your goals you must maintain the intensity. This builds up momentum and gives you the best chance of reaching your full potential.

I believe that life is a process of constant pushing. *Keep On Pushing* speaks to the idea of persevering, being persistent, never giving up. It is impossible to achieve high-level success without meeting opposition, without having to face a 650-lb. sled at the start of your journey. Success dictates that you keep pushing these challenges out of the way, or push yourself over the barriers.

Keep On Pushing also embodies the concept of redefining your limits, constantly going beyond what you originally thought was possible, growing, striving to reach your full potential and embracing change. It is this aspect of *Keep On Pushing* that I would like to focus on next.

Revisiting the house I grew up in on Sunrise Drive in Olympic Gardens. Seven of us lived here.

CHAPTER 1

Enlarge Your Vision of What's Possible

*"We all have possibilities we don't know about.
We can do things we don't even dream we can do."*
Dale Carnegie - American Writer and Lecturer

Human beings are designed and created for great success. Deep in our core lies an innate and powerful desire for full expression of our abilities. There is a seed of greatness in everyone, and each person is at least remotely aware of the incredible things they could do with their lives. This is why we live so vicariously through our heroes – star athletes, pop icons, Hollywood celebrities and so on. Observe children at play, or daydreaming. They all imagine themselves as someone great. A superhero, a famous actor, a stellar athlete. I have never seen a child at play pretending to be an ordinary Joe. I suspect that children have always been this way, but technology, economics and social factors prevented most from pursuing their visions of greatness. Unfortunately, after they outgrew the Superman cape, many of these kids allowed themselves to be saddled by a very limited view of what is possible in their lives, and never adjusted their self-imposed limitations, even into adulthood. Today, the opportunities exist for everyone to use their particular mix of talents and attributes to achieve something great in life. Despite the evaporation of trillions of dollars from the stock market, there are still more self-made millionaires than there were five or ten years ago. In every area of human endeavor – science, business, art, politics, sports – people are soaring to heights never before imagined. Yet success still eludes many.

Unfortunately, they have succumbed to the challenges of life, and have settled for just getting by. You have the ability to join the ranks of those who have found success and happiness. You have the ability to achieve far more than you have achieved up to this point. All you have to do is **Keep On Pushing** beyond the status quo. It is almost criminal how far below our full potential many of us live our lives. We have allowed the circumstances of our birth, society, and the economy to determine the level of our success. I believe that those excuses are almost laughable today. No matter your circumstances, there are many with similar conditions who found a way to rise above them. The great "secret" to their success, and yours as well, is this: It doesn't matter where you are coming from. All that matters is where you are going. Neither your past nor your current situation has to be equal to your future. Renowned American psychologist Abraham Maslow said, "People have a tendency to settle for far less from life than they are truly capable of." Many are stuck in dead end relationships, grappling with floundering businesses or twirling their thumbs in dead end careers when they should be moving rapidly onward and upward.

The goal, the singular focus at the top of a bobsled track is to have the fastest start. A fast start gives the team a reasonable chance of winning the race. Granted, the team still has to negotiate the rigorous turns up ahead, all of which present their own unique set of challenges. But that is simply accepted as the price you pay to reap success. The push is key, and at the start of every race you can hear coaches and supporters shouting, "Big push! Big push!" egging their team on and getting them juiced up for this important part of the race. And even though the push is only used to describe what happens at the start, the driver must **Keep On Pushing** during the run. Hanging back, as I used to do in my middle distance races, and going for the big kick at the end is not a luxury he can afford. He is constantly pushing himself to the edge of his abilities to get the sled down the track as fast as possible. In the bobsled race of life, the individuals, companies and organizations who continue to push hard after overcoming the initial inertia at the start are those who often enjoy meteoric rise and success. Although we have the ability to deliver that big push, not everyone does, nor maintains the intensity.

NON-STARTERS
In life there are many who simply refuse to turn up at the start. Their only focus is on how difficult the track is. They limit themselves by fearing the crash: the chances of the business failing, getting passed over for the promotion, being hurt in a relationship. They worry about being ridiculed or criticized by others, or a myriad of other things that could go wrong. These folks abandon the hope and the promise that life offers. They sit back and watch those who have the courage to go for the ride surge ahead. Unmotivated, uninspired, they do just enough to get by.

JOGGERS
Joggers take to the start, but instead of pushing with all their might, they choose instead to jog – to take their time. They surmise that if they leave the top of the hill with less speed, they minimize their risk of crashing. They want to play it safe. Unwittingly, they don't realize that the track doesn't care how fast

you are going. Each turn is still perilous. Foolishly, their effort is half-hearted at best. Their input on the job is lackadaisical; their indifference in their relationships glaringly obvious. They refuse to do anything to improve their current level of skill and make very little effort to expand their point of view. They, and others like them, live by the mantra "at least we tried." They find a comfortable place where they can "skate by" and essentially choose mediocrity. Like non-starters, they live compromised lives, hanging on to the illusion of what is, instead of striving for what could be. They have no vision.

PUSHERS

These are the people who approach life with a "balls to the wall" attitude. They are not content living life vicariously through their heroes. While they may look up to these people, they acknowledge that they are made of the same stuff and have the same potential for greatness. Unlike non-starters and joggers, who constantly take an inventory of their shortcomings, pushers refuse to allow what others may consider a disadvantage – race, gender, age, family background or any other obstacle – to stand in their way. These obstacles do not intimidate them. On the contrary; they attack them with a sense of urgency, and use them as fuel to propel their success. Pushers are possibility thinkers. They dedicate themselves to a lifetime of growth and achievement.

CHAPTER 2

Push Past
Your Limitations

"Push yourself again and again.
Don't give an inch until the final buzzer sounds."
Larry Bird - American Basketball Player

I believe that we are born with that desire to charge down the bobsled track of life looking for ways to go faster and improve our time. We hate quitting or settling for a place that is unworthy. Every one of us has the capacity to dream grand dreams, which in turn inspire us to constantly push towards higher levels of achievement. Although these things are inside all of us, they do not just bubble up to the surface on their own. They have to be nurtured and developed.

I spent my early years, from seven months old until I was about four years old, with my grandmother in the rural district of Haughton, in the southwestern parish of St. Elizabeth – about seventy-five miles outside of Kingston. Some of my most vivid memories are of the stories she used to tell me about soldiers. Soldiers could perform these amazing physical feats and were always pushing the envelope of their physical abilities. Her stories fired up my young imagination, and although, in my child's mind, I had strong reservations about being able to jump from multi-story buildings without breaking my legs, I knew I wanted to be a soldier. In high school, I discovered that you could enlist in the Army as an officer. It seemed like a daunting task, but I decided that that was what I wanted to do. To do that meant staying in school and getting good passes in the General Certificate Examinations (GCE) and the Caribbean Examinations Council (CXC) in the 11th grade. GCEs are exams handed down from the University of Cambridge and Oxford that students throughout the English-speaking Caribbean take at the end of high school. Students throughout the United Kingdom take these same exams as well. CXC was the Caribbean version of the English exams. By the time I took them, they were only in their second year of phasing out the GCEs. Students, on the strength of these passes, can enter the job market or go to college.

Succeeding in my GCE and CXC exams, although a huge accomplishment, was only the first step in an Army career. I had to go through a "selection board," a rigorous three-day selection process similar to the Army Officer Selection Board used by the British Army to select its cadets for the Royal Military Academy Sandhurst. In November, 1984, six months after graduating from high school and unsuccessful in finding a job until I got into the Army, I reported to Up Park Camp – the Army base in Kingston.

Thirty-three of us turned up that morning, and by mid-day, after a series of interviews and medical assessments, we were whittled down to only nine. By early evening we were on a truck heading up to Newcastle. Newcastle is the Training Depot of the Jamaica Defence Force. The base was founded in 1841 by Field Marshal Sir William Gomm, who, incidentally, is the longest serving soldier in Britain. Field Marshall Gomm was an ensign at the age of ten and Constable of the Tower of London over eighty years later at the time of his death in 1875.

In the 1840s, Up Park Camp and the other Army barracks located on the Liguanea Plain in and around Kingston were being ravaged by yellow fever. On average, one soldier died every two and a half days. Field Marshall Gomm believed that a mountain station could effectively combat the effects of the disease, and so he relentlessly badgered the War Office in London until they acquiesced. The British government purchased a coffee plantation protruding from the southern face of the grand ridge of the Blue Mountains, and Newcastle became what is believed to be the first permanent mountain station in the British West Indies. Shortly after the camp was established, deaths from yellow fever fell precipitously.

Despite its long and storied history, the thing that strikes you first about Newcastle is its beauty. Nestled in the Blue Mountains – home of Jamaica's world famous Blue Mountain coffee – the camp offers a clear view of the city of Kingston and a spectacular view of the seventh largest natural harbor in the world.

As part of the Selection Board's requirements, we had to give both an impromptu and a prepared speech, and complete a leadership task as well as a physical test in the form of an obstacle course and a long run. Our first morning in Newcastle saw the nine of us standing in an extended line on the obstacle course being given our instructions.

At the time, that was the most important test of my life, and I knew my dream was in sight if I could *Keep On Pushing*. The atmosphere was really intense. They knocked us off balance with the almost ruthless way in which they conducted the first part of the selection, and have managed to keep the pressure on us ever since. The green Army coveralls we were issued offered little protection from the cold winds blowing off the Caribbean Sea. I don't know if I was shivering because of the cold winds or because my nerves were so frayed.

As I stood there shaking like a leaf on a windy day, I noticed a captain walking down the steps leading to the obstacle course.

He looked so powerful and self-assured. I imagined that not so long ago he was standing where I was, feeling as frightened and vulnerable as I was, and now he was strutting around like a demigod. I decided that if he could do it, then I could; and from that moment on, I knew I would be fine.

In the end, I was the top pick of only three who were selected. Six months later (including eighteen brutal weeks of basic training), I was an officer cadet at Sandhurst, where I received a Queen's commission on December 13th, 1985.

My military career did not get off to the brilliant start I anticipated. I really struggled during the first twelve to fourteen months. A severe shortage of officers resulted in a heavy workload, and the fact that I wasn't as organized as I should have been resulted in me not being as effective as I could have been. My company commander and I had a mutual dislike of each other. He didn't like me because I was from the ghetto, and I disliked him because he stifled me. As I struggled to get my career on track, I constantly felt as if I was locked in a maze and couldn't find my way out. I kept running into dead ends and had to retrace my steps only to find myself hopelessly lost again. The walls of the maze kept moving. Every time I thought I was going to make a breakthrough with my work, the rules of the game changed. There was no consistency. What was acceptable to one of my superiors was absolutely unsatisfactory for another. What one superior would rake me over the coals for, another officer would get a pass on.

I was in a real quandary. My Army career felt like it was on life support, and at that point I had no idea what I would do if my career came to a premature end. Even as I worked to improve my performance, I knew I needed another goal to pursue. I needed something to get my juices flowing and to take my mind off the difficulties I was experiencing in the Army.

I remember the moment as if it were yesterday. I was walking down to the Officer's Mess and I began asking myself, *what now?* I was twenty-one years old and had achieved my life's ambition. Was this it? Was this all there was for me? I would have given anything to become an Army officer, and given my background, the challenges I faced and the obstacles I had to scale to get there, I had achieved greatly. But there had to be more. I loved Army life, but something deep inside told me that there was more to my life. It was during this moment of introspection that I experienced one of those *ah-ha* moments and I revived my secret ambition to become an Olympic athlete.

In high school, I had aspirations of competing in the 1984 Olympic Games in Los Angeles. As far as I knew, a high school athlete had never represented Jamaica at the Olympic Games, and I wanted to be the first. It never happened. The Olympics came and went, and I was not any closer to achieving that goal. I graduated from high school and enlisted in the Army that year. It was now 1987. The Summer Olympics were coming up in Seoul, South Korea, and I figured that if I got fit enough I would have a shot at representing Jamaica. I started my training in earnest, running five miles every morning before reporting for duty.

That summer, in 1987, exhausted from a long stretch of duty, I ran a cross country race and finished fourteenth from a field of forty. I was way off Olympic pace, but unbeknownst to me I had caught the eye of a few people, including my commanding officer, Colonel Alan Douglas.

A few weeks later, I was on duty at the Battalion Headquarters when the duty clerk walked in with a big stack of mail. I reached in and pulled out one piece. It was the *Force Orders*, which is essentially a weekly newsletter that detailed the happenings in the JDF. Scanning through it, I didn't notice anything unusual until I got to the section on sports. In part that section read:

A.

Applications are hereby invited for personnel who wish to be trained for possible selection to represent Jamaica at the Winter Olympics to be held in Calgary, Canada in February 1988.

B.

Applicants must be in very good physical condition and be wiling to undergo hard and dangerous training.

It actually took me a few readings to figure out that Jamaica was about to start a bobsled team. My first reaction was not unlike that of many people around the world – one of incredulity. Do they know how dangerous that sport is? How would the team train? I doubt that I gave much thought to the fact that the Olympics were less than a year away. After I got over the initial shock I knew I wanted to be part of the team, but I had no idea how I was going to pull it off. I didn't think I was fit enough.

My morning runs were interrupted by duties, so I pushed to get them started again. At the time I did not understand the concept of explosive speed – getting to top speed quickly – so I trained the only way I knew how – I ran. I ran hard and pushed myself harder and harder trying to get in shape. Even though I was training so hard, I wasn't sure that I would even get a chance to attend the team tryouts. There was a distinct possibility that I could have been scheduled for duty that day, and duties take precedence over everything else.

My big break came one day while I was at work. My commanding officer was passing by my office when he called out to me. This made me nervous. The last time he called me over in such a fashion was the week before the cross country race, and I ended up on the duty roster for seven consecutive days, with each tour of duty lasting twenty-four hours. That is what you would call cruel and unusual punishment. This time his instructions were decidedly different and would impact my life in ways I couldn't have imagined at the time.

"I want you to go out for the bobsled team trials," he said. It seemed like an afterthought – an idea that popped into his head as he was passing my office.

The colonel was not an athlete, although it was fun to watch him put his old soccer moves on display during the occasional match-ups between officers and sergeants. He was a sports fan who hailed from the coastal town of Falmouth, about sixty-five miles from Kingston. Falmouth is the capital of the parish of Tre-lawny, which was best known for its sugar estates and sugar fac-tories. Now it is known for its yams, since its favorite son, Olym-pic champion and 100m and 200m world record holder Usain Bolt, jokingly attributed his athletic prowess to them. It is the birthplace of other Jamaican Olympians too, including Beijing 200m Champion Veronica Campbell-Brown. It is also the birth-place of Canadian sprint star Ben Johnson and Voletta Flowers, mother of the late rapper and hip hop icon the Notorious B.I.G.

I don't think I fully appreciated the magnitude of the achieve-ment of competing in the Olympics at the time. Sure, I fulfilled a childhood dream of becoming an Olympian, and did it in a way that was historic, but in one sense it was like just another tour of duty in the Army. Despite all the accolades and attention, I did not see myself as a star. I was just doing my duty. After each bobsled trip overseas, I would literally exchange my bobsled uniform for my Army uniform and go right back to work.

To illustrate: Almost seven months after the Calgary Games, on September 12th, Jamaica was slammed by Hurricane Gilbert, a powerful Category 5 storm. The eastern end of the island was devastated. That night I found myself on patrol on the streets of Kingston with about twenty soldiers from my platoon. As we proceeded down a main road in an area called New Kings-ton, I heard chattering coming from one of the premises which was surrounded by a ten-foot wall. I lined my men up against the wall and went up to the heavy metal gate to peer into the dark interior. Before I knew it, a shot ricocheted off the gate just above my head, and by the time I could take cover behind the wall several more shots rang out. In between the shouting and the shooting, I realized that we were being fired on by security guards from the American Embassy. I didn't even know that those premises belonged to the U.S. Embassy, and it was clear that these guards were scared out of their wits. After a few tense minutes, I was able to calm the situation down, lucky to walk away with my life.

During the last few days of the Games in Albertville, in 1992, unknown to me violence and tension had flared up in the garrison communities of Rema and Tivoli Gardens in Kingston. In early February, Mark "Jah T" Coke was killed as a result of a dispute between rival gangs. His father – Lester Lloyd Coke, also known as Jim Brown after the famed American football player – was also a tough gang leader with strong political ties. The older Coke was in jail awaiting extradition to the United States for his role in a number of murders, drug trafficking and other gang-related crimes. But before those proceedings could have been completed he was mysteriously burned to death in his jail cell. It occurred on the same day his son was buried.

When I returned to Jamaica, the troops were deployed around Kingston and, naturally, I traded my bobsled uniform for my Army uniform and joined them. On my second night back in Jamaica, I led an operation into the Maxfield Avenue area. I was on the second floor of a burned-out building overlooking Maxfield Avenue with one group of soldiers positioned to my north and another just south of my position. I had received information that gunmen used one of the gullies in the area as their attack and escape routes. At about three a.m. I noticed a group of about six men crossing Maxfield Avenue. They all had rifles and were moving towards the rear of the group that was to my south. I immediately got on the radio to alert the sergeant leading that group. By the time I could complete my radio transmission gunfire broke out, and by the time the shooting died down I was unable to raise the sergeant on the radio. The large open lot between my position and the sergeant's was strewn with mounds of garbage and dirt. It was pitch black. As I crawled over to his position, shouting out the sergeant's name, I was quite aware that one of the gunmen could have been lurking behind one of the mounds of dirt. I paused briefly to marvel at the kind of life I led. Only a few days earlier I was at the Olympic Games on television in front of the entire world, and tonight I could be shot and killed in a nondescript, garbage-strewn lot in a Kingston ghetto. In the end, one of my soldiers was grazed by a bullet and one of the gunmen killed.

UNLOCK YOUR POTENTIAL

A few months after the Calgary Olympics, the team began to make a series of public appearances across the United States on behalf of the Jamaica Tourist Board. It was during those trips that I began to notice that there was a big wide world beyond the Army and that somehow it was possible for me to participate in it. Through bobsledding, I began to see that the world was full of opportunities – but more importantly, that I was full of potential.

The biggest lesson I took away from the experience of competing in Calgary is not that I can learn to push a bobsled in a relatively short period of time and become proficient enough to compete in the Olympic Games. What I treasure most from the experience is the knowledge that human beings can achieve anything they set their minds to. The fact is that you and I have more innate potential than we could use if we lived several lifetimes. I have heard it said that if you could run at a hundred miles per hour in the direction of your potential, you would never be able to come within miles of it. That means that whatever you have accomplished so far in your life pales in comparison to what you have the ability to do. When you strive to unlock your potential you will always raise the bar on your performance; or if the market-place raises the bar, you will be able to respond successfully.

As you know, the high jump is a field event in which competitors must jump over a horizontal bar placed at measured heights without the help of any devices. Although it probably occurred in the Olympics of ancient Greece, the first recorded high jump event took place in Scotland in the 19th century. That unknown jumper cleared a height of 5'6". Early jumpers used a method known as the "scissor kick." This technique required the jumper to approach the bar diagonally and kick one leg up and then the other in a scissoring fashion to get over the bar. The technique had its limitations, as there was only so high you could go. Irish-American M.F. Sweeney developed the "Eastern Cut-off." By starting as if he was going to do the scissors kick and then extending his back and flattening out over the bar, Sweeney achieved a more economic clearance and set the world record at 6'5 1/2" in 1895.

Next came the "Western Roll," developed by another American, M.F. Horine. Using this technique, the bar again is approached on a diagonal, but the inner leg is used for the take-off, while the outer leg is thrust up to lead the body sideways over the bar. Cornelius Johnson won the 1936 Munich Olympics using this technique, and set a new world record of 6'8". Innovative jumpers kept on pushing, or in this case, literally raising the bar. They modified the Western Roll by adding a bit of speed and developed what was known as the "Straddle Technique." As a result, by 1957 the world record was quickly raised to 7'. Once again, this technique proved limiting.

By 1967, the landing surfaces used in the high jump were higher and softer. American Dick Fosbury took advantage of this by adding a new twist to the outdated Eastern Cut-Off. He directed himself over the bar head and shoulders first, sliding over on his back and landing in a fashion which would likely have broken his neck in the old sawdust landing pits. The "Fosbury Flop," as it was appropriately named, was a far more effective way of clearing the bar, and Dick Fosbury went on to win the gold medal at the 1968 Mexico City Olympic Games. Every high jumper now uses the Fosbury Flop, and it has been used to break the world record and push the limits of the sport several times. The current world record is held by Cuba's Javier Sotomayor. In 1993, he cleared an amazing 8'1/2."

The history of the high jump demonstrated an interesting and instructive trend. Every time the bar was raised, someone developed a new technique to get over it. This speaks directly to you and everything about your life, business, career, and family. The skills you developed yesterday will limit your potential and hence what is possible in your life the same way those earlier jumping techniques limit the heights to which those jumpers could reach. *Keep On Pushing* raises your expectations to become a better person, parent, spouse, manager, leader, and citizen.

CHAPTER 3

Six Ways You Can Keep On Pushing

"To be what we are, and to become
what we are capable of becoming, is the only end in life."
Robert Louis Stevenson -
Scottish Novelist, Poet, Essayist and Travel Writer

Here are six ways in which you can *Keep On Pushing*:

KOP ONE:
PURSUE EXCELLENCE
In a bobsled competition, the race often continues long after the winners have been declared and, in some cases, the medals have been presented. Interestingly, despite this fact, I have never seen any of the remaining teams approach their runs with a nonchalant attitude. You can easily make the case that completing the race is a mere formality, since the winners have already been declared. However, what I have observed instead are individuals pushing and racing with the ferocity and intensity of a team within striking distance of winning gold and setting a record.

You must give your absolute best effort every time. You have to be willing to push a little harder and to reach just a little beyond where you are right now. Even as the last team approaches the hill they know that the medal winners have already been decided. And though they don't stand a snowball's chance in hell winning the race, they still put in a gigantic effort because they are striving to improve on their last performance and to create new personal benchmarks. This is what peak performers do, and how they *Keep On Pushing*. This is the hallmark of excellence. Aristotle said it best when he declared, "We are what we repeatedly do. Excellence then, is not an act, but a habit." When you get in the habit of being excellent at what you do, you raise your own level of expectation and are therefore able to reach beyond. In pursuing excellence, you find yourself on a continuous journey. Not pursuing perfection, but rather seeking constant improvement, learning and developing new skills, and satisfying an innate desire to explore our full potential. As the American educator and novelist John Gardener points out, "When we raise our sights, strive for excellence…we are enrolling in an ancient and meaningful cause – the age long struggle of humans to realize the best that is in them."

Keep On Pushing is an ongoing journey and is never an end in itself. The pursuit of personal high performance is the source of tremendous pleasure and gratification. It is the feeling an athlete experiences in victory, a salesperson gets when they reached a quota or a student when they ace an exam. Performing at peak levels is not simply about winning or being number one. It is about pursuing your personal best.

KOP TWO:
CHOOSE CAREFULLY
In order to fully experience this incredible journey called life, you should carefully choose to set compelling goals. Goals act as a conduit for your energies and abilities. They engage your subconscious mind and create and attract the circumstances needed for their attainment. They push you out of your comfort zone

and cause you to stretch beyond your perceived limitations. Living without clear goals is like driving your super fast sports car in a thick fog. Despite its potential to perform at a high level, you are forced to drive slowly, tentatively making very little progress on even the best roads. Choosing clear goals burns away the fog, instantly allowing you to step on the gas pedal of your life and charge rapidly towards becoming who you can be.

While goals open up your eyes and mind to the opportunity for you to succeed, that opportunity itself does not guarantee achievement. It will not present your goals to you in a neatly wrapped package ready for you to enjoy. Opportunities always turn up in work clothes. They present a chance for you to run, lift weights, study, research, go through a training program, develop new habits – in short, grow, so that you can explore your potential.

One shortcut to *Keep On Pushing* and becoming excellent at what you do requires you to carefully select your pursuits. Reaching for the stars in your life's pursuit, whatever they might be, involves you having to be willing to pay any price, go any distance and invest any amount of time necessary. Making that kind of effort is easier if you are pursuing something that you thoroughly enjoy. If you try to work at something you don't enjoy or don't believe in you'll never be happy, and you'll never be successful. Having clear goals and working on the things that best suit your talents and interests motivate you to push harder. Unless you really care about your work, you will never be motivated to persist and achieve higher levels.

KOP THREE:
TAKE CONSISTENT ACTION
Action is the bridge between goals and their achievement. No matter how great your aspirations, your chances of realizing them without taking action are as good as trying to win the lot-

tery without buying a ticket. High achievers take massive action in order to unlock their potential. Since winning in any area of life requires you to play full out, you totally immerse yourself in what you need to do in order to win. This means that you become disciplined, and this forces you to do what should be done even when you don't feel like doing it.

We live in what I like to call the microwave society: Everyone wants to enjoy immediate success and be an overnight sensation. Truth be told, the vast majority of those who are enjoying "instant" success endure long periods of sustained effort in order to reach that level of accomplishment. It is consistent action blended with other characteristics (among them intelligence, skill and luck) that gives you the highest probability of unlocking your full potential.

KOP FOUR:
PRACTICE CANI –
CONTINUOUS AND NEVER-ENDING IMPROVEMENT

During one of the public relations trips we made on behalf of the Jamaica Tourist Board in 1988, we had an opportunity to attend a Lakers Game at the old Forum. While there, we met Mike Tyson. Mike had made history himself. He had defeated Jamaican Trevor Berbick to become the youngest heavyweight boxing champion in history. In the ensuing months and years, Mike became invincible. Every opponent who faced him met certain annihilation. Then came Buster Douglas. He was fully expected to meet the same fate as his predecessors, but instead he knocked out "Iron" Mike. The not-so-surprising reason for this is the fact that Mike Tyson had become complacent, and complacency breeds failure. He figured that he had reached the mountain top and he was now untouchable.

Mike was not like the East German bobsled team. In November, 1989, I was in Austria. It was my second week as a bobsled driver and I was in the warm house calming my nerves before I took to the track. Above the hum of the activities I heard someone exclaim, "My God, they've changed the start again!" The person was referring to the new start technique the East Germans were using. Superior engineering had already given them some of the best sleds on the circuit. They were among the top athletes in the world, and certainly enjoyed a fine bobsled tradition. However, they were not content with their past success. They kept tinkering with and tweaking what they had in order to get better. The next time the East German team was called to the starting blocks, all eyes were trained on them.

The starting block is simply a piece of wood cemented in the concrete of the track. Similar to starting blocks in track and field, the brakeman places his feet on it in order to get a better start. The piece of wood is long enough so that the side pushers on the four-man sled can also use it. Customarily, the brakeman *controls* the push. The rest of the crew waits for him to set the sled. Most brakemen place one foot on the ice with their heel up against the starting block. The point on the ice where the back of the sled meets his toe becomes the set point for the sled. Once the brakeman sets the sled, the driver adopts his starting stance, digging his spikes into the ice and grabbing the push bar firmly. Timing is very important, so the brakeman and driver spend hours working on the start in order to get the timing down.

The technique the East Germans introduced saw the driver placing one of his feet on the starting block and the other dug into the ice. Once the sled is set and the team is ready to push, the brake-man explodes on the sled while the driver pushes off from the starting block and sprints forward to the push bar. With this technique, not only does the driver hit the sled with forward momentum, but it also eliminates the need for the perfect timing which the other technique requires. The East Germans were not satisfied with their past success. They kept on pushing, and today most of the bobsled world uses the technique they first showcased in 1989.

Tiger Woods was the same way. You may remember when he won the 1997 Masters at Augusta National by a record twelve strokes. Shortly afterwards, he retooled his swing twice. Many thought that it was totally unnecessary, almost silly, for Tiger to change his golf swing. He was regarded as perhaps the greatest golfer of all time, and many experts thought his swing was as close to perfection as any one was going to get. But Tiger was obsessive about improving his game. In an interview with Ed Bradley on CBS's *60 Minutes*, Ed asked him why he changed his swing. His answer came back quickly: "I wanted to get better."

Ralph Waldo Emerson once said, "Unless you try to do something beyond what you have already mastered, you will never grow." The truly great ones know this. In the 1960s Muhammad Ali floated like a butterfly and stung like a bee. He danced around the ring and skillfully avoided his opponent's best shots. However, in the 1970s, he stood toe to toe with them and willingly traded punches in order to get the win. Michael Jordan added a fade away jumper to his repertoire late in his career after he was no longer able to take off from the foul line. After his eight gold medal performance in Beijing, Michael Phelps is now experimenting with a new freestyle stroke.

During their recovery from World War II, several Japanese companies implemented a philosophy known as *kaizen*. Kaizen, the Japanese word for improvement, focuses on continuous improvement throughout all aspects of life. When applied to the workplace, kaizen activities continually improve all functions of a business, from manufacturing to management and from the CEO to the assembly-line workers. For example, at Toyota, engineers would push a perfectly good assembly line until it broke down and then find and fix the flaws. Like kaizen, *Keep On Pushing* embraces the philosophy of continuous and never-ending improvement in all aspects of your life. It rejects the complacency that Mike Tyson and many others demonstrate in their lives. Whether it is bobsledding, golf, playing a musical instrument, studying, or being a parent or a spouse, the same process of continuous learning and improvement of performance applies.

KOP FIVE:
EMBRACE CHANGE

If there is one thing that you can be sure of, it is that change will happen. It is a natural, inevitable part of life, and remains one of the most important factors affecting our lives today. Perhaps more than at any other time in human history, the speedy infusion of new ideas, knowledge, products and services is creating unprecedented and amazing possibilities for everyone. Apart from being the natural order of things, why is change taking place at such an alarming rate? It is because some individuals decided to *Keep On Pushing*. They are always looking for better, faster, more efficient ways to do things. They are relentless in pursuing their own potential, and that is reflected in the ideas that they conjure up and the things that they do. The high achiever knows that growth is a precursor to success – and that growth occurs only when you are willing to embrace change and move out of your comfort zone.

In 2000, digital music players were either big and clunky or small and useless, with equally terrible user interfaces. On October 23, 2001, Apple, Inc. launched the iPod, which went on to become the best-selling digital audio player series in history. At the time, most MP3 players used controls that were better suited to the Sony Walkman in 1979. Instead of using skip buttons, a user could spin a wheel on the front of the device to scroll through a list of songs to find the one they wanted to play. The same wheel was also used to control the menus of the system. As a result, it was much easier to navigate through the iPod's playlist than the comparable Nomad or Compaq MP3 players. Since the release of the initial iPod with a capacity of 5 GB, Apple has created an entire family of iPods to include the iPod Mini, Nano and the iPod Touch, which are much smaller but equipped with capacities of up to 64 GB.

The need to embrace the inevitability of change is true for our personal lives as well as for our professional lives. It applies to individuals as well as multi-billion dollar corporations. Successful people, whether they be entrepreneurs or executives, students or teachers, trades-people or professionals, are always learning and developing new skills, and thereby having a much greater chance of remaining relevant in this increasingly competitive world. Successful companies are invariably those that research and develop new products and strategies and implement new systems. These companies, and the people who make them up, are motivated at every level to step out of their comfort zones, to be open to fresh ideas, to allow themselves to see the possibility of change. As the historian Eric Hoffer wrote, "In times of change, learners inherit the Earth, while the learned find themselves beautifully equipped to deal with a world that no longer exists."

KOP SIX:
TAKE PERSONAL RESPONSIBILITY

People have a tendency to readily accept responsibility for things that are going well in their lives and abandon responsibility for the things that are going unsatisfactorily. They blame their bosses, their parents, their spouses, the economy and anyone else they can find for things that are less than ideal in their lives. What they fail to realize is that this level of thinking is restrictive and prevents them from employing all their faculties to overcome the challenges facing them. To paraphrase Albert Schweitzer, *Keep On Pushing* means that you stop attributing your problems to your environment and once again learn to exercise your will, your personal responsibility. It means that you stop making excuses for your perceived shortcomings and constantly work to strengthen your areas of weakness.

When you *Keep On Pushing* you are empowering yourself. You cannot control everything that happens to you, but there is no better feeling than knowing that you have the power to control your own destiny. As Elaine Maxwell said, "I am the force; I can clear any obstacle before me or I can be lost in the maze. My choice, my responsibility, win or lose, only I hold the key to my destiny." The successful ones understand that, through free will, they can choose to take actions which will create the kind of results they desire. Setbacks and challenges are viewed as opportunities for personal development, allowing them to become stronger, wiser, more knowledgeable and more skillful. Taking personal responsibility is the price you pay to achieve the greatness you are capable of.

KEY POINTS TO REMEMBER - LESSON 1

- You will always have a bag of plausible excuses for not achieving your goals. You either produce excuses or you produce results. You cannot do both. When you **Keep On Pushing** you eventually produce the results you desire.

- High achievers use the challenges they face on their way to their goals to feed their hunger. They develop a need to prove to themselves that they can achieve their goals. They know that success doesn't come cheap, and so they make sacrifices and endure all kinds of difficulty in order to achieve it.

- Persistence forces you to think outside the box and to come up with creative ways to achieve your goals.

- No one is immune from challenges, setbacks, weaknesses and liabilities. Do not use them as crutches. Work through them with the attitude that it is impossible for you to fail.

- Your first actions might not be successful. Oftentimes, you have to go through a learning curve as you work to achieve your goals. Goal achievement is like problem solving. Problems are often solved through persistent trial and error.

- Lack of persistence is one of the biggest reasons for failure. People simply give up, and once you've given up you've accepted defeat. Sometimes things simply will not go your way, but if you don't quit you must achieve your goals.

ASSIGNMENTS

1. Take an inventory of your life (skills, accomplishments, possessions, etc.) to establish a baseline.

2. As clearly as you can, from the vantage point of your baseline, define what you would like your life to be.

3. Commit yourself and begin to do everything in your power to transform the image you have described into your new baseline.

4. Repeat number two. Remember to go as far as you can see, because when you get there you will see further.

"Gentlemen, this is a bobsled." Coach Howard Siler bringing us up to speed during our first trip to Lake Placid. Sept. 1987. (**Left to right:** Devon Harris, Michael White, Dudley Stokes, Howard Siler, Samuel Clayton

Bobsledding Jamaican style: Practicing our starts on the Army base in Kingston. Oct 1987.

Persistence Pays

"If I had to select one quality, one personal characteristic that I regard as being most highly correlated with success, whatever the field, I would pick the trait of persistence."

Richard DeVos - Co-Founder of Amway

Whenever I give autographs, I always write a little message before I sign my name. I feel that a few words of encouragement or inspiration are worth more than just a signature scrawled on a piece of paper. I agree that it does take more time for me to do, and adds to the length of the line and the amount of time I actually spend giving autographs. But I do it anyway. I think it is worth the effort. In 1988, my favorite thing to write was, "keep on keeping on." I didn't realize it then, but I was telling people and reinforcing in my own mind what I was subconsciously telling myself all along, "keep on keeping on!" The journey might be tough, but hang in there! Don't give up!

As you can imagine, the effort and the process for getting to the Olympic Games for any athlete is no walk in the park. That was especially true for us. Not only were we undertaking something that had never been done before, we were doing it under the constant glare of the media and the most trying of circumstances. No matter what, we had to keep on keeping on. The good name of our beloved island nation was at stake. We simply could not give up.

CHAPTER 4

Strive For Excellence, Not Perfection

*"The essence of being human
is that one does not seek perfection."*
George Orwell - English Novelist and Journalist

With a seating capacity of 35,000, the National Stadium in Kingston is smaller than many college stadiums in the United States. Built for the 1962 Central American and Caribbean Games, it is the stage for most of the major sporting events on the island, including the annual Inter Secondary Schools Sports Association (ISSA) Boys' and Girls' Athletic Championships. Simply known as "Champs" among the locals, the event is a veritable showcase of young athletic talent and a rich source of recruits for scouts representing American universities. Champs began in 1910 and has become the proving ground for all of Jamaica's Olympic athletes. In 1981, I entered Champs with big goals: win gold in the under-seventeen boys' 800m and 1500m races, and break the meet and national record in the latter. Despite nursing a strained hamstring, which I'd suffered three weeks earlier, I brimmed with confidence that my goals were well within reach. In addition to bringing glory to my school, winning would mean a spot on the Junior National Team to compete in the CARIFTA Games. The games were being held in Bermuda that year, and that would allow me to fulfill another secret wish – to travel overseas. Of course, there was the possibility that I would catch the eye of an American scout, but I wasn't interested in a track scholarship. The only thing that I wanted more badly than winning those races was to enlist in the Army and attend Sandhurst.

I was just settling into third place with a smile on my face during the first 100 meters of my 1500m heat when I felt a bump on my right heel. One of the runners behind me had stepped on my heel and, out of the corner of my eye, I saw my spikes flying across the track. I have no idea why I didn't continue to run. After all, I spent my early days in high school running barefoot. Instead, I dashed across all eight lanes to edge of the track to get my shoe and put it back on. By then the rest of the field had opened up an insurmountable lead. I completed the race, but my dream of winning gold and breaking the record had evaporated. The 800m event was my last chance to win gold, and after I had cruised through my heat and made it to the finals, it had seemed likely. But, as they say; "if I knew then what I know now."

I was really motivated to achieve the goals I had set for myself. One of the techniques I used to increase my motivation was my insistence that I wanted to win gold – and no other medal would do. That really motivated me to train hard, but it also proved to be my Achilles' heel. I insisted that if I realized I wasn't going to win the race that I would start jogging to ensure that I finished outside of the medal standings. I was going for perfection – gold or nothing at all. Of course, with my failure to even make it to the 1500m finals, my perfect little picture was becoming undone; but I was still adamant that I would settle for nothing but a gold medal.

I made some slight technical errors near the end of the first lap, and by the time I reached the back stretch with 300m to go, I somehow convinced myself that I was too far behind to win the gold medal that I so yearned for. I started jogging and, to my surprise, even fifty meters from the finish line, runners were still zipping past me. I was much closer than I believed. It was a foolish strategy, and it taught me a very painful lesson that day. My "gold or nothing" attitude was an imprudent attempt at perfection. I believe that as human beings we are flawed in so many ways that it is nearly impossible to be perfect – yet we can always strive for excellence. Excellence simply means trying your utmost best every single time. Unlike perfection, excellence is always in sight and, because it is, you are more likely to continue to try hard, to dig deep, even when the odds are against you. And, in so doing, sometimes you will actually find perfection. If only I had strove to do my utmost best in that race, no matter how it looked at the time, I might have won it.

Six years later I was back at the stadium to take part in another important athletic event. The stadium is an impressive building. Its huge columns outside the grandstands, not to mention its importance in the life of our nation, in a strange way brings to mind the Roman Coliseum. As I approached the grandstands, I passed the statue of Dr. Arthur Wint, the first Jamaican to win an Olympic medal. He captured gold in the 400m event at the 1948 Summer Games in London. Known as the "Gentle Giant," the statue showed him bolting out of the blocks with his trademark long strides. Next to him was a much shorter man, Donald Quarrie. Many said that he was too short to effectively run the corner in the 200m and would therefore never become a champion. He responded by winning gold at the 1976 Montreal Olympics. At the time of his victory, Jamaica was just converting to the metric system, and one of the slogans they used to help us remember the units of measurement was "Donald Quarrie...world beater in meters." I wouldn't come to understand the importance of the Olympics and the significance of Quarrie's victory until almost four years later.

As I walked past the statues commemorating these two Olympic greats on that September day in 1987, they seemed to be saying to me, "Don't screw it up this time." They didn't have to remind me. I had learned my lesson well, and although I wasn't bubbling with confidence the way I was six years earlier, I was determined more than ever to make the team.

About forty of us were ushered into a small room among the offices atop the grandstands. There, we were given a brief talk about bobsledding and shown some of the equipment used in the sport. Of course, it made sense to wear a helmet, and for the first time I was feeling the smooth, sleek lycra material that made up those skin-tight suits bobsledders race in. The spikes they used on the ice were specifically made for the purpose, with scores of small teeth placed a millimeter apart. They were so sharp I cut my fingers on them.

Most of the guys who turned up for the team trials on the second day were track stars from the Army. I had watched many of them dominating the track during the various Army track meets. There is no doubt that I was fit. I was what I called Army fit, not sports fit. For the previous two years I was engaged in Army training. I had logged a couple hundred miles walking up and down the Blue Mountains, around the Jamaican country-side, across Salisbury Plains, the South Downs and other Army training grounds around England. I had run dozens of miles around Barossa, a vast wooded area behind Sandhurst, often with more than fifty pounds on my back and a rifle in my hands. I was in great physical condition, but that didn't necessarily translate into me performing at a high level on the sports field. It is similar to the NBA player who has been out for a few months because of an injury. Although he may have undergone some intense workouts after his rehab to prepare him for competition, when he returns to playing he is just not as sharp. You will often hear coaches and commentators say that there is a marked difference between the conditioning and fitness that you get from practice as opposed to that derived from being in a game. At the bobsled team tryouts, I was going up against the best that the Jamaica Defence Force had to offer to win one of the precious few spots on the bobsled team. My lack of sports training while I was going through my Army training put me at a significant disadvantage.

Some of the events have changed over the years, but at the time it was the same test the United States and other established bobsled nations used to select their teams. They included sprinting 30m, 60m, 100m and 300m, throwing a shot putt from between the legs, doing five consecutive standing broad jumps, a standing high jump, power cleans and a push test with a makeshift sled. They were designed to test explosive speed and power. Once again, I was at a disadvantage. Coming from a middle distance background, my body was conditioned for endurance and stamina. In fact, the only part of the test I was comfortable with was the 300m run because I did those for speed work. Winning one of the four spots seemed impossible, but I was determined to pull it off. Interestingly enough, I discovered after the trials that my commanding officer didn't expect me to make the team. One of the philosophies in the Army is that officers must always participate. I happen to agree with it. It is good for morale and demonstrates good leadership because the troops get to see the officer working hard and giving his best. Since the Colonel had a number of enlisted men trying out for the team, he thought he would send his young fit officer as well. Chris Wilkie, another officer, was also instructed to attend the team trials. He was a sky diver, and since bobsledding is kind of an adventure sport, the Colonel thought Chris would be a suitable candidate. The

Colonel didn't expect him to make the team either, and Chris dropped out midway through the first day.

Each participant had as many as three attempts at each test. The best performance was given a score and matched up against the others. The fledgling Jamaica Bobsleigh Federation had brought two guys from the United States Bobsled Team to administer the tests. Michael White, a radio operator in the Army Reserves, was clearly the fastest of the group. He breezed through the short sprints. I was mentally keeping score, and surmised that I was hovering around fifth place. I was doing everything I could to get into the top four. As expected, I did well in the 300m run. During the trials, most of the group kept together. I stayed a few feet away from everyone, but close enough to hear instructions that were being given out and also to eavesdrop on the conversations. I figured I might be able to pick up a tip or two that could help me in the trials, but I mostly kept to myself. Even with everyone scurrying around me and moving from one event to the next, I wanted to have some quiet time. I was building up an unspoken determination to make the team, and even when I felt like I didn't do well enough on a particular test, I resolved to do much better on the next. At the end of the first day one of the Americans smiled at me and said, "You had a good day today."

On the third day of the trials we did the power cleans and the push test. I didn't know anything about bobsledding, but I knew that if there was one test that had to be pre-eminent, it had to be the push test. It was done under the grandstands using a makeshift sled on wheels. I was once again determined to make my mark. And I did. I ended up with the two fastest pushes. And the American guy smiled at me again and said, "You had a good day today!"

CHAPTER 5

Overcoming Inertia

*"So many fail because they don't get started - they don't go.
They don't overcome inertia. They don't begin."*
Ben Stein - American Actor and Writer

I had expended so much physical and mental energy during the team trials that I was totally exhausted. Once they were completed, I went back to my room in the officer's mess and crashed. I don't remember waking up even once during the night. During breakfast the next morning my friends began calling me, "The Olympian". Apparently, while I slept the night away, it was announced on the sports news that Jamaica now had a bobsled team and I was named as one of the team members. I was very encouraged by the news, but was careful not to get my hopes up too high. I needed to get some official word first.

Confirmation of my selection to the team did not come until a few weeks later when I was given an airline ticket and told I was going bobsledding. When I arrived at the airport, I saw three other guys that I recognized from the team trials. Three of us were Army personnel. I was a lieutenant and platoon commander. Dudley Stokes was a captain and helicopter pilot. As I expected, Michael White was also selected to the team. He was a private and a radio operator. The lone civilian on the team was Samuel Clayton, an engineer with the now-defunct Jamaica Railway Corporation. Our first trip was to Lake Placid, New York to meet our coach, Howard Siler. Howard, I believe, was an insurance salesman, but at the height of his bobsled career competed on the American bobsled team and had a respectable fifth place finish in the two-man event during the 1980 Winter Games in Lake Placid.

It was during that weekend trip that we saw a bobsled track for the first time. It was a massive, winding concrete structure. The Lake Placid track was originally built for the 1932 Olympic Games. At the time it was 1.5 miles long, but was later shortened to a mile and used for the 1980 Games. A few years after we got into the sport, the track was banned from use in international competitions. The long straightways made it too fast and unsafe for modern day sleds, which were significantly faster than the sleds back when it was built. With walls that towered almost twenty-five feet above us, the track was at best intimidating. They have since built a new, safer track, and the old one is now used for tourist rides during the summer using sleds on wheels. That weekend, we also saw a bobsled for the first time. It was a crude, tiny lump of fiberglass mounted on a metal frame. The fiberglass hull, or cowling, as it is called, is closed in the front and open in the back. On the front left-hand side is a collapsible push bar for the driver. The four-man sled also has two collapsible push bars in the rear. These are used by the side pushers. The push bar for the brakeman is fixed. Until the 1960s, the drivers used a steering wheel to steer the sled. Today, drivers pull two D-rings which are attached to a rope-and-pulley system that connects directly to the front axles to which the front runners are bolted. In theory, steering a bobsled is quite easy. You pull on the left D-ring to go left and right to go right. The front runners can only move three inches to the left or right. The challenge with driving a bobsled has to do with timing and intensity. The best drivers know exactly when to steer the sled and how much pressure to apply to the steering. The longer rear runners were fixed. I was having difficulty visualizing how anyone could get in one of those things running as fast they were going downhill. What was even more harrowing, though, was imagining the sled traveling at such high speeds and still negotiating the track, especially the tight spaces between the straight ways and the corners. The brake was located in the back of the sled. It is simply a rake underneath the sled attached to two levers situated either between the brakeman's legs or up against the side of the sled. The brake is applied only in the braking stretch – after the sled has crossed the finish line. The brakeman simply pulls up on the lever and the rake digs into the ice and snow to slow down and eventually stop the sled.

While in Lake Placid we went over to a local ice rink to train with the American team, who were practicing their push starts. In fact, it was the same rink on which the "Miracle on Ice" took place in 1980, where the American ice hockey team defeated the Soviets in a startling upset. Now we were in town to perform a miracle of our own. The Americans were kind enough to lend us some old ice spikes, and taught us the push technique. Although this was our first time pushing a real bobsled, the first time we were seeing more ice than what could fit in a tall glass of lemonade and we were nowhere near mastering the techniques, the competitive juices began to flow. We wanted not only to put on a good show but to also beat the Americans. Thoughts of a grand, impressive entry into the sport quickly gave way to the harsh reality of how difficult the road ahead was going to be for us. We watched the Americans dart across the ice as easily as a sprinter tearing up a running track while we shuffled, slipped and skidded around the rink.

This bobsled idea was no longer merely difficult. It was darn near impossible. We spent more time that day picking ourselves up off the ice than actually pushing the sled. Nonetheless, we kept on pushing, we kept on keeping on, and not only did we learn to walk on ice, we eventually learned to run on it really fast as well. In fact, we learned so well that by the third heat of the four-man event in Calgary, only a few months later, we posted the seventh fastest start time. If my memory serves me right, there were twenty-eight sleds in the race. Pretty good for a group of guys who, a few months earlier, couldn't even walk on ice, wouldn't you say?

More than twenty years after Calgary, people are still surprised that our team was formed. Some still think the idea hilarious, and I am still asked the same set of questions: How did guys from a tropical paradise get involved in a sport like bobsledding? Who came up with the idea? How did you practice? How did you manage in the cold? They still view our team in a light-hearted way; however, there is nothing light-hearted about bobsledding. Notwithstanding the fact that you could get killed or seriously maimed, bobsledding requires a high degree of discipline, dedication and hard work.

In 1996 we were in Calgary, preparing for the 1998 Nagano Olympics. We wanted to use the push track, but it was covered under about eight inches of snow which had fallen the day before. The push track is a practice track where teams practice and perfect the push technique, especially during the summer. The work crews at the Canada Olympic Park, where the push track was located, were busy clearing the roadways, and so clearing the push track was very low on their list of priorities. Rather than wait around with the hope that they would eventually get to the push track, we got shovels and brooms and spent more than an hour clearing the snow so that we could have a 30-minute training session.

That same day, a local newspaper wanted to do a story on us. The photographer thought that a shot of us riding in the sled grinning from ear to ear, armed with shovels and push brooms, would be great for his newspaper. We respectfully declined. All he could see was the mistaken zany, happy-go-lucky view that people have of us. He was totally oblivious to the commitment and dedication it took for us to clear the track. There were other teams who wanted to use the push track that day, but we were the only ones who chose to undertake the laborious task of clearing the snow. It is true that the idea of our team is a most unusual idea – far outside of expected norms – but we demonstrated that such ideas not only have merit, but that through common sense, persistence, brainstorming and getting creative, you can turn such ideas into reality.

The idea of our team was birthed by two Americans, George Fitch and William Maloney. They both lived in Jamaica and had business and family connections there. The story they like to tell is that they wanted to test the notion that Jamaica had some of the best athletes in the world and figured that a good way to test the ability of an athlete is to see how well he can adapt to a new sport. They chose bobsledding because of the push cart derby in Jamaica. It reminded them of bobsledding. The Jamaican push cart is a wooden box cart. It has four wheels that are made of wheel bearings wrapped with old tire rubber. The steering mechanism consists of an old car steering wheel attached to a piece of iron for a steering column. They wrap a piece of rope around the steering column and attach it to the front axles of the cart. For brakes, they use a piece of tire rubber nailed to the back of the car. In true Fred Flintstone style, whenever he needs to stop, the driver, who is to the rear of the cart, steps on the rubber and it rubs along the road until the cart stops. The carts are used to sell wares in the market-place, and every year they are spruced up and raced down a winding mountain road. It is a popular event, but not every Jamaican can say they have pushed a push cart. Over the years, only one of our team members, my brakeman, Ricky McIntosh, has ever participated in the push cart derby.

On the surface, the push cart derby is a lot like bobsledding minus the ice, although, in my mind, it is a lot crazier. These daredevils tackle hairpin turns at about 40mph. Imagine how painful it would be skating across asphalt at such speeds. A really ugly sight. The other reason they chose bobsledding was because the start is such an important part of the race. They needed sprinters, and in Jamaica they figured they could get the pick of the litter. However, the guys on the summer team wanted no part of this harebrained idea and left George and William scrambling for other sources to find athletes.

It requires a lot of pushing to overcome the inertia of a stationary sled. It is often difficult to get people to buy into new ideas. People often resist ideas that are against accepted norms with such fervor you would think their lives depended on it. They scoff and criticize them, and like the guys on our summer team, although talented and possessing the skills needed to take advantage of the new opportunity, will flatly turn them down simply because they are new. Some of the most successful ventures, and certainly things that are now a fabric of our everyday lives, were initially seen as far-fetched ideas when they were first hatched. Months after Orville and Wilbur Wright's father, a Methodist minister, declared that only angels could fly, they achieved flight. I've heard that Henry Ford's banker refused to finance his efforts to develop the motor car. He didn't think anything would replace the horse and buggy. We now know how far off the mark both these gentlemen were. Sometimes we come up with innovative ideas, but because they cut so deeply against the grain we fail to pursue them.

Fortunately George and William didn't behave that way. Rejected by the guys on the summer team, George approached the Army.

Colonel Ken Barnes was in charge of sports in the Army at the time. In his younger years, Colonel Barnes was an avid athlete, representing Jamaica in soccer and obviously passing on those genes to his son, John Barnes, who played professionally for Liverpool and also represented England in the World Cup. More importantly, the Colonel was a guy who thought outside the box and immediately saw the possibilities. Without his support, I believe the idea of the team would have most certainly died. I remember him telling me that it was a wonderful chance and that if he was twenty years younger he would have pursued it himself.

CHAPTER 6

Enduring In the Face of All Difficulties

"Difficulty, my brethren, is the nurse of greatness – a harsh nurse, who roughly rocks her foster-children into strength and athletic proportion."

**William Cullen Bryant -
American Poet, Journalist and Editor**

George Fitch and William Maloney thought that several corporations would immediately see the unique marketing opportunities offered by the team and sponsorship dollars would be rolling in. Their assumptions were wrong, and things took a turn for the worse with the stock market crash in October, 1987. George and William were bankrolling the effort and had sustained substantial losses in the market. At the time, the four of us were sharing a hotel room in what had to be the cheapest, sleaziest joint in all of Calgary. I had a bed to myself, and Dudley bunked on a sofa-bed while Michael and Sammy shared a bed. George came over for a team meeting and painted the grim picture for us. We could go back to Jamaica and wait for corporate sponsorship to come, or we could stay in Calgary with almost no money and slug it out. The more logical, comfortable choice of the two was to go back to Jamaica and wait for the money.

At first glance, that seemed like an easy decision to make. We had no funding and, as it turned out, second only to the equestrians, bobsledding was the most expensive Olympic sport. We needed money for meals, hotel rooms, practice runs, gym memberships and so on. It made sense to go back to Jamaica and wait until we got sponsorship. At the very least, it gave us a reasonable way out if the effort failed. If we failed, we could claim that it wasn't our fault. We didn't make it to the Olympics simply because we didn't have the funding. I am sure you can see that that in itself is faulty thinking, and if you are engaged in that kind of thinking you should stop it immediately or suffer the consequences of being left with a big bag of plausible excuses but no accomplishments. As they say, "You can either produce excuses or you can produce results. You cannot do both." When you *Keep On Pushing* you eventually produce the results you desire.

Remaining in Calgary was definitely the more difficult option, but there is often no easy way to your goals. We elected to stay and fight, and it was at that very point that the future of Jamaica bobsled was sealed. More than twenty years later, Jamaica still has a team that is vying for the Olympics. We know now that, had we gone back to Jamaica to wait for the avalanche of corporate sponsorships to come in, we would still be waiting. None came.

The decision to stay meant that we had to endure several hardships and one of the thoughts that constantly percolated through my mind was the motto of the Jamaica Defence Force Training Depot: *"No obstacle too difficult, No task too great"*. It was prominently displayed above the parade square in Newcastle, and I read it practically every day. Whenever the challenge of turning our dreams into reality seemed daunting, I reflected heavily on those words.

I remember after one particularly difficult day of training having only a chicken leg, a roll and a small soda for dinner. In Igls, Austria, we stayed at the Landesssportheim – a sports hostel near the center of town. They had much nicer accommodations than the Panama Motor Inn where we stayed in Calgary. The rooms were cleaner, much better laid out and instead of all four of us cooped up in one room, we were two to a room. They served a continental breakfast, but that left us ravenous again by mid-morning when we were ready to go to the track , just a few miles up the hill in the neighboring town of Igls.

The first morning we tried to take a roll and a few slices of cheese with us to the track. The attendant accosted us. She was a rather large, imposing lady. "Vat are you doing?" she asked. "Zat is not allowed," she growled, causing us to shrink at least two inches. After that, we always ate an extra roll for the road.

I am often asked about what drove and pushed us through those difficult times as we worked towards competing in Calgary. The answer is that we were hungry! As a 21-year-old burning up so much energy during the day, I had a huge appetite and my stomach often growled with hunger pangs. But that is not the kind of hunger I am referring to. We were hungry for success. We could fulfill a lifelong ambition to compete in the Olympics, the chance not only to represent our country with honor, but also to add to our rich sports heritage, and the desire to be the best bobsledders we could possibly be drove us constantly.

In order to excel in sports, business and life, you must have the fires of ambition burning within. You must be hungry for success. High achievers use the challenges they face on their way to their goals to feed their hunger. They develop a need to prove to themselves that they can achieve their goals. They know that success doesn't come cheap, and so they make sacrifices and endure all kinds of difficulty.

PERSISTENCE
PROMOTES CREATIVITY

When you *Keep On Pushing* you are bound to come up with some creative ways to get to your goal. Persistence forces you to think outside of the box, whether you are working on raising capital for a new business venture, solving a supply issue in your company or creating a better work environment in your office. You cannot engage in and employ the same level of thinking that you are accustomed to. As Hannibal, the great military commander and tactician known as the Gifted Strategist, is credited with saying, "We will either find a way, or make one." He is reputed to have marched an army of 38,000 infantry, 8,000 cavalry, and thirty-seven war elephants from Iberia over the Pyrenees and Alps into Northern Italy, at one time breaking through a rock fall with vinegar and fire in order to do so. It seems that there is always a way to achieve your goal. Your job is to find it.

With no sponsorship deals on the horizon, a strong desire to move forward, and the pressing need for funds threatening to derail our efforts, we knew we had to find alternate ways to get funding. After a lot of cajoling George Fitch agreed to print t-shirts. I really wanted us to include the phrase "The Hottest Thing on Ice" in any design we came up with, so every time I broached the subject about t-shirts I mentioned the phrase. I wish I could take credit for coining the phrase, but I can't. On our way to the track in Calgary, we had to pass a billboard. It depicted a huge machine driving across some ice with the same phrase. I later learned that the machine was a Zamboni, and it was obviously driving across an ice rink. I liked the phrase and thought that it described our team, so we adopted it.

We literally had to sell the shirts to eat. I can still remember pulling up at a night club with a bag of shirts under my arm, dancing up to a couple on the floor and saying, "Hey mon, wanna buy a shirt?" It is clear now that I needed a better sales pitch.

Most times the guy would decline to buy but the girl would want a shirt, so the guy ended up paying and we got dinner. Sounds like a fair exchange to me.

During the Calgary Games, we spent an hour on the push track before official Olympic ice training.

The Big Push:
At the start with Michael Morgan during the 1998 Nagano Olympics.

CHAPTER 7

Bounce Back From a Setback

"Life is a series of experiences, each one of which makes us bigger, even though sometimes it is hard to realize this. For the world was built to develop character, and we must learn that the setbacks and grieves which we endure help us in our marching onward."

Henry Ford -
Founder of the Ford Motor Company

K*eep On Pushing* is resisting the temptation to quit even after you feel tired, frustrated, exasperated or have been dealt a crushing blow. It is toughening yourself mentally, emotionally and physically. It is keeping your eyes on your goals. It is keeping up the exercise and diet programs. *Keep On Pushing* is keeping up the training, keeping up the studying, keeping up the working. *Keep On Pushing* means being tough on yourself and not accepting excuses even if they are believable and easy to come by. It means continuing to give it your best effort even when you don't see the returns and the results. James Collins, in his book *Good to Great*, puts it this way: "You must maintain unwavering faith that you can and will prevail in the end, regardless of the difficulties, **AND** at the same time have the discipline to confront the brutal facts of your current reality, whatever they might be."

When I first started in the sport, Samuel Clayton, the lone

civilian on the team, and I formed a two-man team. I believed that Sammy and I had the potential to be quite good. I certainly believed that we could have been the better of the two Jamaican two-man teams. We easily out-pushed Dudley and Michael at the start, but they consistently beat us to the bottom. Dudley was driving better than Sammy, and Sammy was frustrated. He wanted us to push even harder. Since we were not yet the fastest starting team on the ice, I was certainly interested in faster start times as well, but Sammy was clearly missing the point. Any improvement in our finish times on the track was dependent on his ability to learn the lines – the fastest path around each corner – and improve his ability to drive the sled. No matter how hard I tried to coax and encourage Sammy, I couldn't get him to put more effort into learning and mastering the drive-lines. His approach was to push the sled as fast as possible, hit every wall in sight and see where the clock stops. That attitude is a recipe for frustration and failure in any venture. You must have the discipline to make the effort to learn the basic skills. You cannot hope to improve without first laying the ground work on which you can build. A bobsled driver who doesn't take the time to learn his lines will be no more successful than a pharmacist who doesn't understand chemistry or a sea captain who doesn't know how to read his charts.

I was getting frustrated as well. Sammy had developed a reputation for his lack of concentration, and became the butt of a few jokes around the track. One day, after we had just completed a training run in Calgary, Sammy went over to one of the track workers and reported that he noticed a goloshin in the track between corners eleven and twelve. Goloshins are rubber shoe covers that we place over our ice spikes to protect them when we are not on the track. They are usually removed and placed in the sled just before we are ready to push off. The Canadian driver who had come down right after us overheard Sammy and was startled. He hadn't seen the goloshin and remarked that it could be a potentially dangerous situation. It didn't take long for some comedian to change Sammy's story. The "new" story was that Sammy noticed a size ten left-foot goloshin in the track. It had some of the guys literally rolling on the floor in laughter. To the uninformed, it would seem that if Sammy could discern a size ten left-foot goloshin going at almost 80 mph it meant that he had great powers of observation and that would bode well for bobsledding. The opposite is quite true. Bobsledding is so intense, and your mind so focused, that you are not able to see anything except the corners. It is so fast that if you find yourself consciously thinking about what you are supposed to be doing you are likely to crash.

His lack of focus was a real concern for me and it often resulted in us having some very heated conversations, many bumpy rides down the track and even a few crashes. We had one particularly spectacular crash which, thankfully, was not caught on film. It was really embarrassing. It occurred in Igls, Austria. We had just finished arguing, as we so often did, with me demanding that he focus more. The run was going just fine until we got to corner number eight – the Kreisel. The Kreisel in Austria is a particularly high corner. In fact, it is so high that there is a part of it that the track crew does not even bother to clean. "Why?" you ask. The answer is quite simple, really – you have no business being on that part of the track. We were probably traveling 65 mph as we approached the corner. With my head buried in the bottom of the sled as we entered the corner, I felt when the sled rose. Although the brakeman isn't watching, his body is in tuned with the rhythm of the track and he can tell where the driver has steered the sled on each corner. It is not uncommon, especially for inexperienced drivers, to miss the "take on" to the curves and cause the sled to go too high on the corner. In this case, I thought we were a little high but assumed that Sammy had things under control. My assumptions were way off. The next thing I knew the sled spun around in the air, fell to the bottom of the track and started going down the track backwards. Evidently, we went so high that the front of the sled hit the frost line. When that happened, it slowed the front of the sled down. With the back of the sled traveling faster than the front, it caused the sled to spin around. I put the brakes on and stopped the sled in the next corner. Needless to say the track crew was not happy. The brakes are never applied on the track because they dig up the ice and result in the track crew spending extra time to repair something that they spent hours shaving and spritzing to make as smooth as possible for race day. Of course, for the next week or so the other teams had a good laugh as well.

Things came to a head the following week when, after our usual argument, we started down the track. Again, it was a routine run until I found myself literally on the top of my head, my butt off the seat and the bottom of the sled kissing the skies going more than 70mph. That did it. We weren't unionized, but I went on strike. I decided that I would rather return to Jamaica than slide with Sammy ever again.

As a result, George decided that I should try my hand at driving, since I had expressed an interest. I was scared to death, but I went out to the track to kick start my bobsled driving career. Right after I completed the track walk, the heavens opened up and ten inches of snow fell, closing the track for the day. It was then I decided that I should team up with Dudley. I was adjudged to be the better brakeman and Dudley the better driver. Michael and Sammy would now be a team. There was no further talk about me driving that season.

When we got to the Olympics in Calgary, we were still working overtime. At this stage of the game, we should have been on a training regimen that would help us to maintain our conditioning and keep us sharp, but we were still training as if it was still the mid-season. Before going to the ice track for official Olympic training, we spent at least an hour at the push track. During the training sessions on the ice, my push times were much slower than I thought they would have been. I didn't realize it then, but I was pushing with tired legs on account of all the training we did on the push track before. The day before the Olympic race, Dudley decided that Michael and I should have a "push off" to see who would compete on race day.

Each team got two runs during the training session, so Dudley decided that Michael would push on the first run and I would push on the second. The person with the faster push would be on the sled with Dudley come race day. Dudley promised to push as hard as he could for both of us. That day we skipped the training on the push track and headed straight to the bobsled start. Michael pushed a fast time on his run. Faster than anything I had done in training. But I was up the task. I immediately started warming up and inside I had built up a resolve that I had never felt before. I was up to the challenge. When they returned to the top, I went over to help Michael with the sled and to congratulate him on his push. To my surprise, Howard, the coach, called me aside to say that Dudley wanted to go with Michael on the second run.

I was crushed. Failure is a difficult pill for me to swallow, but if I have given it my all and still come up short, I can find a way to live with it. Part of the success game is acknowledging that sometimes your best might just not be good enough. In those instances you learn your lesson from the experience and move on. But this was different. The agreement we had with Dudley was for Michael and I to lay it all on the line. The person with the better performance would compete in the race.

Instead, in one selfish, unethical moment my dreams were dashed. If Michael had beaten me in a head-to-head push off, I would surely have been disappointed. But such is the nature of sports. The same is true in business and life as well. You match your performance against the next guy and if his is better, he is declared the winner and you accept that, at least on this occasion, he is better. I thought of challenging Dudley, but the soldier in me and a desire to see the team get the best result possible prevented me. I did not want to be a distraction at this critical point of our journey. Sacrificing my personal ambition for the good of the team was very painful, but the team and the country had to come first. With this in mind, I supported them with the same intensity I would have had if I were on the sled.

With this disappointment behind me, I turned my attention to the four-man competition. Caswell Allen was slated to push on the right and sit in the second seat behind Dudley. Michael was on left as the number three guy, and I was pushing from the back as the brakeman. On about the second day, Chris Stokes joined our practice sessions. Dudley gave me the responsibility to teach him everything I knew about pushing a bobsled. Chris was having a very difficult time getting in the sled from the side. It can be very unnerving pushing a sled and then, while running at top speed down hill, jump on a ledge that is probably no wider than the palm of your hand and in one clean movement get over the side of the sled and sit down without bumping the sled to one side or the other. It had to be especially intimidating for Chris, who, until a week before, had never seen a bobsled. What I didn't realize until several years later was that all along Dudley had planned to have Chris on the sled.

The perfect break came when Caswell fell on the push track. Although the injuries he sustained were no more than a few scrapes and a bruised ego, George Fitch declared him too hurt to compete. Caswell played into their hands because the night before he and Freddy Powell broke curfew. We had to be in bed by nine p.m. every night, but he and Freddy decided to sneak out and enjoy some of the Calgary night life instead.

Now at this juncture Chris was not even a member of the Olympic delegation, let alone an athlete on the team. I suspect that George was able to use a few bottles of Jamaica's fine Appleton rum to persuade the Olympic Officials to give Chris the necessary accreditation. With Caswell declared hurt, Chris officially replaced him.

This occurred three days before race day. I gave up my spot on the back of the sled so that Chris could push from there. It was much easier to get on the sled from the back. To my surprise, on our last training day, almost on a whim, it seemed, the coach decided that there was one spot up for grabs on the sled and Caswell and I should fight for it. It was shocking to me that after I had worked so hard, and was slated to be the brakeman on both the two- and four-man sleds, I was in danger of being relegated to the role of spectator with a grand view of the Olympics. Caswell was presumably so hurt that he had to be replaced by Chris, and overnight he was fit enough to be challenging me for my spot on the sled. As taken aback as I was with the sudden turn of events, I didn't spend any time lamenting over it. I had every intention of being in that race. At least this time I had a chance of deciding my fate. Just as with the two-man, we were down to the last two runs. And once again, the decision was made for Caswell to go first. It was Dudley driving, Chris on the back, Michael pushing from the right and Caswell pushing on the left. I don't remember their start time, but I believed that the team could push faster with me on the sled. I was still in a state of shock, but at least this time I was going to get my shot. As I got ready to take my place on the left-hand side for the second run, Howard told me that I should switch places with Michael and push from the right. That was one of those "what the fuck?" moments, but I chose not to waste any energy by dwelling on it.

"Back set!" Chris shouted.

"Set!" Michael, myself and then Dudley called.

Chris chimed in, "Two, three, four!" and we exploded on the sled and rocketed down the track. I was pushing as hard as I could. I had only one shot and I had to make it count. Of course, I had no idea what my time was, but that was all I thought about on my ride down the track. It was the end of the training session, so there was no need to go back to the top of the track. As we packed away the sled in the storage bin, Howard came by and told me that I would be on the sled on race day.

Perhaps the biggest setback we faced as a team in 1988 was the crash on the third run of the four-man competition – it was seen and heard around the world. We never once believed that we didn't belong in the sport. But with this spectacular crash it seemed we had given credence to our detractors. We were disappointed and upset with ourselves for making this happen. The press was hounding us for an interview, and George Fitch asked me several times to go speak to them. I said I would but never did. I just did not know how to face the world and talk about one of my biggest failures.

It is really interesting to note how others have sought to look at our performance in Calgary almost from a perspective of lowered expectations. Time and time again I've met people who would say that our team did exceptionally well to make it to the Winter Olympics even though we were from the tropics. In their eyes, just being at the Olympics was an extraordinary achievement in itself. While there is a lot of truth to that and we are exceedingly proud of our achievement, our mindset was decidedly different. We didn't view our liabilities as excuses for poor performances. We believed that, although we were from Jamaica, we had the ability to perform at a world class level, and so we pushed ourselves to do exceptionally well despite the obstacles.

No one is immune from challenges, setbacks, weaknesses, and liabilities. However, too many people use them as crutches. They frame their performance and anticipated success with the challenges they start out with. Most assuredly, with that attitude they are already defeated. You have to go after your goals as if there are no limitations and it is impossible for you to fail. You have to know that no matter where you find yourself – in the midst of a financial meltdown, health challenge, a relationship crisis – you can always make it through and take yourself to the next level.

It would have been easy for us to have quit then. People probably would have said, "They did well. It was a good effort. We understand." Even as we were experiencing our greatest setback, we knew we would bounce back. If you take into account our accomplishments in the sport in the ensuing years – 14th place in the four-man event in Lillehammer ahead of France, Italy, Russia and the United States, winning both the men's and women's World Push Championships in 2000 and 2001 and setting the start record in the two-man event at the Salt Lake City Olympic Games – you could make the argument that we did in fact bounce back.

While working to achieve your goal, it is important to acknowledge that most times your first actions might not be successful. There is always a learning curve. Goal achievement is like problem solving. Problems are often solved through persistent trial and error. You simply keep trying different methods until you arrive at a solution. The same is true in goal achievement. Your challenges cannot be treated as dead ends. You have to see them as detours to your final destination. You must be willing to keep changing your approach until you realize your vision. When a person just will not give up – when they are willing to keep going, keep changing their strategy, keep being creative – they eventually find a way. This, by the way, marks the very important distinction between being stubborn and being persistent. A stubborn person will not give up. The grave mistake they make is not changing strategies. They keep trying the same proven, unsuccessful tactics expecting different results. As French author and philosopher Simone de Beauvoir so aptly stated, "In the face of an obstacle, which is impossible to overcome, stubbornness is stupid." Successful people know that there is always a way to win and that it is their job to find it, so they consistently change their approach until they find one that works.

Lack of persistence is one of the biggest reasons for failure. People simply give up, and once you've given up, you've accepted defeat; you've cloaked yourself in failure. No matter your field of endeavor, you will always face obstacles. Things simply won't go as well as you planned or expected, but be persistent, be determined, persevere. I recently came across an interview I did in 1997 with *Sports Illustrated Kids*. In it I stated, "If you don't quit you must achieve your goals." I happen to believe that with all my heart. That's what I kept telling myself as I worked to get to the Nagano Olympics; and, as you know, partly because I didn't quit, I did compete in those Olympic Games and became a three-time Olympian.

After the Albertville Games in 1992, I retired from the Army and moved to New York. My goal was to pursue a degree and a career in hospitality management. It may sound strange to you, but I was trying to leave the bobsled world behind. Bobsledding felt like such a fairytale, and it was time to get back to the real world. In New York, I quickly found a job in a Jamaican restaurant near my home in the Bronx and started part-time studies at the New York City Technical College in Brooklyn.

But the bobsled bug started to bite again and I couldn't shake it. Call me delusional, but I felt I had the ability to win an Olympic medal. I didn't feel like I had gotten a chance to train the way I needed to in order to win in the two Olympics I had competed in. I wanted to win an Olympic medal. Work, school and family life dictated that I missed the 1994 Olympics in Lillehammer, Norway. I would have really loved to have gone, but I knew that it wasn't practical. With the anticipated windfall from *Cool Runnings* not forthcoming, I decided to put school on hold after two semesters and, for the next two years, juggled work, family, finding sponsorship and endless squabbles with the Jamaica Bobsleigh Federation in Kingston.

One of the first things I did when I moved to New York was to form the Jamaica Bobsled Club, New York. My goal was to raise funds and recruit and train Jamaicans who live in the Tri-state area so that the Federation in Jamaica would have a larger pool from which to select its Olympic team. I did this with the blessing of the then-president of the Jamaica Bobsleigh Federation, Leo Campbell. I first met Leo in the JDF, where he also served as an officer. He was Dudley Stokes' peer and attended high school with Chris Stokes. Every conversation I had with Leo had the same rhythm. It would start out with him taking a hard line, but by the end of the conversation he would soften his position and sound more reasonable. To me, it seemed that after we came to an agreement on how to move the New York-based club forward, he would report to the rest of the Federation, which opposed the idea. Like a good soldier, he would then come back to me expressing the views as if they were his. After I gave my counter arguments, he would soften his position, we would leave the conversation agreeing on a way forward, and the cycle would start all over again. By 1996 Chris Stokes had taken over as president and the same dance continued. It was very frustrating, but I kept at it. The Olympics were now just two years away, and if I didn't get back on the ice, my Olympic dreams were going to melt into a fleeting illusion.

Much to my surprise, in November, 1996, Chris Stokes called to say that he wanted me to join the team in Calgary for training. The Federation had the funding in place to make a push for the 1998 Olympics in Japan. He offered me $10,000 (which I could surely use), and the Federation would cover my expenses in Calgary.

After almost four years of working really hard, I was finally at the point where I could meet my monthly obligations without having to rob Peter to pay Paul. By now I had two kids, with another on the way. The money Chris was sending me would not go very far, but I also realized that this was the best chance I had to keep the dream alive. The day I left for Calgary my income went from $35,000 a year to zero. When I got there, Dudley Stokes and the coach, Sam Bock, told me there was no money. While Dudley was there with his four-man crew, I would have to continue to train by myself until they could afford to fly a brakeman up from Jamaica. All of this was slightly unnerving, but I figured I could fix it. All I had to do was find sponsors.

By January, 1997, after dozens of proposals mailed and scores of phone calls made, I still had not secured a sponsor. I can still hear the coach's voice in my head saying, "Devon, if you don't get sponsorship by June, you should quit – you will only be chasing pipe dreams."

Sam was Canadian. He began coaching the team in 1994 and played a pivotal role in the team's 14th place finish in Lillehammer. Sam was overbearing and eccentric, but his knowledge of exercise physiology, sled technology and nutrition made him a valuable asset to the team. I knew he was insulting me, but there was no need to start a fight with him. Instead, I agreed with him and I told him that if I didn't get sponsorship by the end of June, I would quit. I was so sure I would have sponsorship by then, and therefore the entire conversation would have become a moot point. Moreover, I was at the point of no return.

I had no doubt that I could have found a job back in New York but after my debacle at Boys Champs in 1981, I wasn't about to quit now. My commitment was irrevocable. Unfortunately, most people give up on their goals without realizing how close they had come. In the grand scheme of things I don't mind in the least when people like my coach tell me I should give up on my dreams, or they stand in my way of trying to achieve them, as the Jamaica Bobsleigh Federation did in my attempt to compete in Nagano. In the end, all they have managed to do is remind me of my resolve to achieve my goals. As it turned out, June came and went and I was not any closer to securing sponsorship than I was in January. But I kept on pushing anyway. When you *Keep On Pushing*, it means that you are not entertaining failure as an option, and although I did not know specifically how I was going to solve this problem, I knew I had to keep the dream alive. I could NOT quit. The truth is that I do not know how to.

GET LUCKY

By June 1997 I was in Evanston, Wyoming with my two brake-men, Jason Morris and Patrick Robinson. Jason was a helicopter pilot and also a retired captain from the Jamaica Defence Force. Patrick joined the team in 1990 and competed as a brakeman in the 1992 Albertville Games. A local attorney, Paul Skog, or "Bosko" as I call him, thought it would be a great idea to invite the Jamaica bobsled team to train in Evanston. Just fifty miles west of Park City, the venue for the 2002 Olympic bobsled event, Paul considered Evanston "the back door to the Olympics." Paul first contacted Chris Stokes in Jamaica with the idea, but with the Salt Lake City Games more than five years away and the four-man team firmly entrenched in Calgary, Chris, didn't want to have anything to do with it. He passed my number on to Paul, who contacted me. Once again, I was presented with a less than ideal shot: I could go to Evanston, which, on the surface, didn't seem to have much to offer except its proximity to Park City; or I could remain in New York with my brakemen in Jamaica while we waited for sponsorship. I decided that we would move to Evanston, and it turned out to be a win-win situation. They provided apartments for us to live in. We had free access to the running track, weight room and gymnasium at the high school. Local craftsmen constructed a sled on wheels so we could practice our push starts. In return, we got involved in the community, conducting soccer camps, speaking in the schools, participating in civic functions and bringing tons of exposure to the town in the press. Comedy Central, ESPN, TNT, TNN and a whole host of other media, including foreign outlets, came calling. Being in Evanston breathed new life into the effort even as the Jamaica Bobsleigh Federation declined to lend us any support.

A local businessman, Alan Griffin, hired us to work in his pizza shop. Patrick didn't have a driver's license, so he stayed in the store and helped to make the pies, earning himself a new nickname – "Pizzamon." Jason and I did deliveries. We trained almost eight hours a day and delivered pizza at nights. As a middle distance runner, whenever I went for runs I would run as hard as I could at the beginning so that by the time I was ready to head back home or to wherever my starting point was, I was already quite fatigued. During those times I would keep telling myself, "just put one foot in front of the other". The going was always painful and tedious, but I would always make it back. I apply the same philosophy when I am working towards a goal, especially during the trying times. I find a way to do something – to put one foot in front of the other. The going may be slow, tedious, difficult, even frustrating, but as long as I am moving in the direction of my goal I know I will eventually get there.

As if things weren't bad enough, my right knee, which I had injured the November before, was swelling more and more. But with no medical insurance, a cold compress had to do. As you can see, my situation was getting dire. But I kept on pushing. Persistence requires applied faith. You have to believe that somehow or other things are going to work out. **BUT** you cannot just sit around waiting for the missing piece of the puzzle to turn up. You have to constantly visualize the finish line – your goal – and continue working so when the solutions do appear you are prepared to take advantage of them. I continued to train, and three weeks before the Games I signed a sponsorship agreement with a Salt Lake City-based telecommunications company. When I told Paul Skog about my sponsorship deal, he burst out with his trademark, "We're getting lucky, Mon!" My brakeman, Jason, defined luck as where preparation meets a good opportunity. Call it what you will; luck, preparation, opportunity, persistence, I was bound for the Olympic Games in Japan. The grin on my face as I marched into the stadium for the XVII Winter Olympiad clearly told the story.

While in Nagano, after a brief conversation in English, our hosts would always leave us with a parting exhortation – *gambatte*. My understanding is that it is one of the most important words in Japanese education. Literally translated, it means "persevere, never give up." In the West, we would be told "good luck," but *gambatte* denotes far more than luck. It tells us that opportunity is not about luck and that success comes from effort, diligence, and perseverance.

As corny as it sounds, I have found out that it is true; what doesn't kill you makes you stronger. When you are going through challenges in your life, it is like going through a furnace. It melts down everything and presents a situation where you can recast yourself into something better and stronger. Look back at the worst problems you have faced in your life. If you were able to conquer them and not let them to get the better of you, if you were able to extract an empowering meaning from the experience, then you would have been stronger for the experience. Oftentimes our worst problems have sculpted our souls and made us stronger than ever.

I did not take my coach's advice. I did chase my pipe dreams, as he put it. I did not quit. **YOU** must never quit. Go chase your pipe dreams! As Walt Disney once said, "The difference in winning and losing is most often...not quitting." You can have anything you want, provided you want it badly enough and are willing to persist long and hard enough and be creative in trying different approached to find the solutions to your problems. Thomas Edison persevered through 10,000 experiments before he found a way to make the light bulb work. Each single act of persistence builds and cultivates success habits, which lock in deeper and deeper. They strengthen you and increase your ability to persist even more. And once you have developed that reputation as someone who keeps on pushing, no matter what, your success is virtually guaranteed. Persistence pays every time.

KEY POINTS TO REMEMBER - LESSON 2

- *Keep On Pushing* speaks to the need to be persistent in order to achieve your goals, but also embodies the concept of redefining your limits, constantly going beyond what was originally thought to be possible, growing, striving to reach your full potential and embracing change.

- Neither your past nor your current situation has be to equal to your future.

- Non-Starters abandon the hope and the promise that life offers. Joggers find a comfortable place where they can shelter from the challenges of life and essentially relegate themselves to a life of mediocrity. Pushers are possibility thinkers. They dedicate themselves to a lifetime of growth and achievement. *(continued on page 79)*

KEY POINTS TO REMEMBER - LESSON 2

- Your potential is virtually unlimited. You can accomplish far more than you have already have.

- You have the capacity to dream grand dreams, which in turn will inspire and invigorate you to constantly push towards new levels of achievement.

- Goals act as a conduit for your energies and abilities. They engage your subconscious mind and create and attract the circumstances needed for their attainment. They push you out of your comfort zone and cause you to stretch beyond your perceived limitations.

- High achievers take massive action in order to unlock their potential. Since winning in any area of life requires them to play full out, they totally immerse themselves in what they need to do order in win.

- Opportunities do not present your goals to you in a neatly wrapped package ready for you to enjoy. They present a chance for you to develop new habits and skills so that you can grow.

- Successful people embrace change and are always looking for ways to learn and develop new skills, thereby making them relevant in an ever increasingly competitive marketplace.

ASSIGNMENTS

1. Examine the seven major areas where you would normally set goals – financial, career, or business, leisure time or family time, health and appearance, relationship, and spiritual. Ask yourself, "What is not working? How can I improve?" Seek advice from people you trust. Identify the issue that would make the biggest difference on your life and start working on it. Once resolved, begin working on the next one.

2. Set high standards for yourself and make striving to do your best a habit.

3. Take delight in facing new challenges and embrace every opportunity to learn and improve your skills.

4. Change your strategy if you are not getting the results you want.

Pushing Unleashes the Power

"People are always blaming their circumstances for what they are. I don't believe in circumstances. The people who get on in this world are the people who get up and look for the circumstances they want, and if they can't find them, make them."
George Bernard Shaw - Irish Playwright

The familiar voice booms over the loudspeakers. It is clear and distinct, tinged with a sense of urgency and purpose. The athletes on the line switch to autopilot, tightening the chin straps on their helmets, stripping off jackets and insulated pants, exposing their thin, skintight lycra suits. Protection from the elements is sacrificed for aerodynamics as hot steam rise from their bodies and dissipates in the air. Oblivious to the deafening screams of the crowd, they get themselves ready.

Coming to their aid, coaches and helpers in one clean movement pick the sled up off its side and place it into the grooves. With push bars securely locked in place, they take their positions on the starting block, hands firmly gripping the push bar, a fiery stare down the track. Their stoic demeanor belies the turmoil that's raging inside of them as the adrenaline pulses through their veins. Unknown to them, the screaming of the crowds has died down, as they now wait with bated breath for the massive explosion of energy that will propel the sled from its stationary position to almost eighty miles per hour in less than sixty seconds.

The brakeman's voice pierces the cold air, "**BACK SET, TWO, THREE, FOUR!**" The brakeman *falls* into the sled. His knees bent at right angles, his back straight and his arms outstretched behind him, he uses his body like a slingshot, catapulting the sled forward. At the same time, the other three guys recoil and then explode on the push bars, forcing the sled to surge forward with the power of a turbocharged engine. In an instant, all four of them have brought to bear the full extent of their ferocious aggression on the 650 lbs. of metal and fiberglass in front of them. Muscles bulging and contracting. Feet digging and churning. Individual effort working in synergy as they blast through the first thirty meters. It is all in the push. The team's performance at the start accounts for almost fifty percent of a bobsled race.

All things being equal, the bobsled team with the slower push is almost certain to come out on the losing end. A difference of one tenth of a second at the start could mean as much as three tenths of a second at the bottom. In a sport where the difference between winning the gold and finishing completely out of the medal standing could be as small as one hundredth of a second, that's a huge advantage. Overcoming the inertia of a stationary sled at the beginning of the race is a major obstacle. The team's ability to overcome it rests in the power of the push.

In the same way that a bobsled team provides power to the sled through pushing, ordinary people, through their own actions, power their way past the obstacles in their lives everyday. Unlike the bobsled, which will move with the slightest effort because it glides on ice, our everyday obstacles are more stubborn because they are so deeply rooted in our psyche. Daily we come up against the status quo, the accepted norms, the popular perception. Daily, we wrestle with the turmoil of in-the-box thinking. We struggle with self imposed limitations. We tell ourselves we are too short, too tall, too old, too young; that we have the wrong skin color, that were are from the wrong ethnic background, the wrong side of the tracks. The list is endless, and, like the athletes at the bobsled start, we must bring all your energies to bear on these obstacles in order to achieve our goals.

CHAPTER 8

What Is Pushing?

"A desire to be observed, considered, esteemed, praised, beloved, and admired by his fellows is one of the earliest as well as the keenest dispositions discovered in the heart of man."

John Adams -
Second President of the United States

A lthough the bobsled athlete takes great pride in having a fast start, the ultimate goal in a bobsled race is to have the fastest finish time. A fast start does not guarantee you a fast finish, but it is virtually impossible to end the race with a fast finish time without that explosive start. At first glance, the pushing seems to be a purely external event. Power generated by the muscles from the legs, backs, and arms. Brute force propelling the sled over thirty meters of flat ice before gravity takes over.

The ferocity that is on display at the start during the physical act of pushing the sled comes from an incredibly intense internal desire for the athletes to be the best. Craving the chance to win, teams are motivated to give their all at the start in order to gain any advantage they can over their competitors. And even if their final results do not get them on the medal podium, they want the bragging rights for having the fastest pushes. They are motivated by the sheer love of the sport, the competition, and the infectious excitement and intensity that comes with every race. Athletes take a lot of pride in being seen as a world class pusher. They want to be respected for their push the same way that, in basketball, you may have to respect an opponent's ability to shoot a three-point shot. Thirdly, athletes are motivated to push hard to ensure that they do better than they did on their last run. There is a yearning for continuous improvement. Finally, the push is fueled by patriotism – the athlete's desire to bring glory and honor to their country.

The same is true of life. Getting a project started does not guarantee its success, but it is a sure bet that it has no chance of succeeding if the effort is not made in the first place. Winning and performing at high levels require the same level of desire that the bobsled athlete displays at the start. All worthwhile achievement begins with an idea, a dream; but what brings them to life is the fuel of human desire. Desire consumes people with an insatiable appetite for action. When you burn with enough desire, nothing can stop you. The impetus for the push in human beings – the things that motivate and drive us to act – are as varied as the goals we pursue and the obstacles we face. In the final analysis, it comes down to an entrenched desire on the part of all of us to want to be in charge of our lives and to feel that somehow, even in some small way, we are contributing to something beyond ourselves.

The thirst to achieve in sports, in business and in life comes from within. At times, it may appear as if external factors have influenced us and pushed us into action. In reality, these external influences really act as triggers that set off something inside of us. What really drives you and I are the ingrained reasons and level of importance that we attach to our goals and dreams. Your power to push towards those goals and dreams depends on how strong those reasons are, and occasionally, when external influences collide with those reasons, they then become your catalyst and motive for action. Your compelling reasons are the fuel for achievement, and when mixed with action creates combustion, igniting a power in you to push past your obstacles in order to achieve your goals.

Feel the rhythm, feel the rhyme!
The four-man team of Dudley Stokes, Chris Stokes, Ricky McIntosh and Michael White gets ready for action in Albertville 1992.

CHAPTER 9

What Creates The Impetus For The Push?

"Many people think they want things, but they don't really have the strength, the discipline. They are weak. I believe that you get what you want if you want it badly enough."

Sophia Loren - Italian actress

Have you ever wondered what holds us back from pursuing bigger dreams? What stops us from taking a chance on ourselves and our ideas? What makes us bury ideas that would provide financial stability for our families and give us a great sense of accomplishment and satisfaction? What keeps us in that dead end job and prevents us from embarking on a career path that we can be enthusiastic and passionate about? What stops us from implementing the ideas that would have catapulted our businesses to the next level? What is it that prevents us from doing the things that would allow us to enjoy more meaningful relationships? What is it that strips us of our power to live a richer more rewarding life?

The things that stop you from pushing are like a ball and chain around your ankles. It saps the energy and life right out of you. If you are struggling with this, you are probably already aware that it is holding you back. This ball and chain really amounts to a number of habits that you can begin to change whenever you choose to. In the next chapter, we are going to discuss what it feels and looks like to be operating without the weight. For now, let us identify the reasons why you are not living your life more fully. Obviously, you cannot correct what you have not identified. On the other hand, pointing out these perpetrators suggests that if you do their opposite, you will begin to feel liberated and energized to push towards your goals.

NO CLEAR GOALS

In bobsledding, the goal is clear: Get across the finish line with the fastest time. Despite the challenges, it is nonetheless a very clear goal. Since the athletes know exactly what they are working to achieve, there is no confusion about what needs to be done and they are able to focus all their energies on the specific steps needed to be taken. Being clear about what they are working towards provides energy and drive.

Unfortunately, in the bobsled race of life, many people spend their entire lives unclear about what it is they want to achieve. Ambiguity leads to confusion and dissipated energy and drive. Clarity makes it easier for you to stay on track and see forward movement, which will motivate you to persist when you face difficulties. With only months to go before the Olympic Games in Calgary, our team was very clear about what we were working towards and that was a huge motivator. Holding a clear picture of ourselves competing in the Olympics allowed us to push until we were finally experiencing that picture in reality.

INABILITY TO RISK SUCCESS

We are all too familiar with the fact that many people are "held back" by the fear of failure, but you would be surprised to know that there are many who are just as intimidated by success. Earlier we discussed the fact that our fears are irrational beliefs that harbor and replay so many times in our minds that they eventually become real. The fear of success demonstrates this quite well. Those plagued with the inability to risk success:

- Fear that they will accomplish all that they set out to, but still won't be happy, content or satisfied with themselves.

- Are afraid that if they succeed, they will be pressured to succeed even more.

- Fear that once they have achieved the goals they worked so diligently for, the motivation to continue will fade.

- Have a fear of being recognized or honored.

- Believe that they are undeserving of all the good things and recognition that comes their way as a result of their accomplishments and successes. They deduce that their accomplishments can self destruct at anytime and they will be replaced or displaced by someone who is better than them.

- Lack a belief in their own ability to sustain their progress, and the accomplishments they have achieved in their life.

Sometimes they convince themselves that by succeeding they are then exposing the inability of their peers to do as well as they do. This is why, month after month, the very capable salesperson might coast so that her numbers are not the ones everyone else on the sales team is trying to beat. Likewise, the talented student might choose to fail so that he doesn't have to live up to the expectations of being the first from his family to graduate from college. Somehow they have lost sight of the fact that we all have a responsibility to work to be the very best we can. Anything less is a sorry waste of the vast potential with which we have all been blessed.

FEAR OF FAILURE

Wherever I go, people always ask me about that spectacular crash that the entire world witnessed live on television during our third run of the four-man bobsled event in Calgary. I have seen the tapes many times, and I must admit that it looked really ugly. But the truth is that I had been in seven crashes that season, and some of the others were worse. A crash is irrefutable proof that a run has failed. One of the goals of each run is to finish it upright on all four runners. Whenever you find yourself upside down, skating on your head at eighty miles an hour, it means that you fell woefully short of the mark.

Bobsledders live with the possibility that they could crash in the blink of an eye. From the minute you jump into a sled, a bobsled run becomes an exercise in dealing with one challenge after another, living on the edge and dancing on the fine line between success and failure. No one is immune from a run turning into a colossal failure. We accept it and push on nonetheless. You risk failure in order to succeed and be at your best. During the times when you do fail, you find yourself with two stark choices: You can stow the sled on the back of a truck and head home, or you can head back to the top of the track and do it again.

Personally, the worst time to crash during a training session is on the last run because it means that I have to wait at least one more day to work on fixing my mistake. As I mentioned, crashing a bobsled is perhaps the ultimate indication of an unsuccessful run, but misjudging the path the sled should take and driving a corner poorly are also signs of failure. Bobsled drivers experience scores of failures during practice. Whether it is an outright crash or a poorly driven turn, they view the event and not themselves as a failure. They constantly work to correct each failure and, in so doing, improve their skills, grow their confidence and become better prepared for race day.

The same is true of life. Those who see failure as final are allowing themselves to get stuck because of one little error in judgment. As a result they give themselves far too little credit. They see themselves as failures instead of seeing the result they got as failure and recognize that they have the ability to correct their temporary lapse. Their inability to tolerate and learn from failure prevents them from pushing and unleashing their power.

FEAR OF REJECTION AND RIDICULE

Don't you remember how people laughed when they first heard that Jamaica was starting a bobsled team? Maybe you were one of them. Many initially rejected the idea of a bobsled team from an island that was better known for its palm trees and sunshine.

We chose not to be so egocentric and recognized that people were rejecting the notion of a Jamaican Bobsled team – they weren't rejecting us personally. We were able to then use this as one of the external factors that motivated us to push past the stereotypical view of Jamaicans. Success at times requires us to be thick-skinned. You cannot afford to take rejection personally or you will never achieve anything in life. No matter how good an idea is there will always be someone who won't see its merits. Guglielmo Marconi's friends wanted to commit him to a mental asylum because he claimed that radio waves could travel through the air. The Eiffel Tower in Paris was built in 1889 as the entrance arch for the World's Fair marking the centennial celebration of the French Revolution. The tower and its engineer, Gustav Eiffel, met with much criticism at the time it was being built. Eiffel was accused of trying to create something that was artistic or inartistic, depending on the person's point of view. The newspapers of the day were filled with angry letters, with many of them calling it an eyesore and a black dot against the beautiful Parisian landscape. Today, with more than 200 million visitors since it was built, the Eiffel tower is the most visited paid monument in the world.

Not only did we embrace the challenge of being the first team from a tropical country to compete in the Winter Olympic Games, in so doing we served as an inspiration to all those who would dare to risk rejection and ridicule – the salesperson who is trying to make quota, the little girl singing solo in the school play, the homemaker who wants to start her own business. Who is to say that our dreams cannot be realized? Where is the proof that is so?

Stop listening to the criticism of others. As Theodore Roosevelt famously said, "It is not the critic who counts, not the man who points out how the strong man stumbles, or where the doer of deeds could have done them better. The credit belongs to the man who is actually in the arena, whose face is marred by dust and sweat and blood, who strives valiantly, who errs and comes short again and again; because there is not effort without error and shortcomings, but who does actually strive to do the deed, who knows the great enthusiasm, the great devotion, who spends himself in a worthy cause, who at the best knows in the end the triumph of high achievement and who at the worst, if he fails, at least he fails while daring greatly."

LACK OF BELIEF IN YOUR ABILITY

As I stand at the bobsled start, waiting to begin my run, there is always an intense internal dialogue going on. The first voice would shout, "Can you do this?" And the second would fervently respond "Yes I can! Yes I can!" I know I can because I have prepared. Hours of training in the weight room, on the running track, ice time and push training have all made me prepared to be standing there at the top of the hill. Certainly, back in 1988, with only a few months of training under our belts, we were not nearly as prepared as our competitors were – but this was not about them. It was about us being able to execute what we practiced and were trained to do, even if it was limited.

It was unlikely that we were going to set any new track records at those Games, but because we had practiced, we knew we could get from the top to the bottom of the track safely, and that belief in our abilities to execute gave us the courage and the determination to push the sled as fast as we could. In the end we did not set any new records, but we pushed off the hill with a very competitive start time. We were at a decided disadvantage when it came to bobsled-specific training and experience, but we had been athletes all of our lives. We all spent years honing and developing our athletic talents in other sports. In part, our success in bobsledding is because we demonstrated belief in those abilities.

If you hope to be your best and reach your full potential, from time to time you will need to embark on a venture that you may not feel you are fully prepared for at the time. And while that may be true, you have to recognize that you still have a lifetime of experiences that you can draw on. There has to be something from your past that you can extract and apply to your current challenge.

So you may be fresh out of college and the only job you have been able to land is one outside of your field of study. If you have learned nothing else in college, hopefully you learned how to learn. You can use those skills to figure out how to perform satisfactorily, and in time master this new job. Just trust in your abilities and take the plunge.

LACK OF PERSISTENCE

We live in what I like to call a microwave society. We expect to have results quickly and without much effort and toil. Unfortunately, life seldom works that way. We have to be prepared to put our shoulder to the wheel and grind it out. We may have had the talent and the ability to become world class bobsledders, but it never came easy to us. It was a long, arduous, sometimes frustrating process – adapting to the life of a bobsledder, all the while keeping our bodies well tuned and our minds sharp and focused. This required a lot of persistence. Persistence is commitment, confidence, desire, discipline, and focus at work.

Your persistence is demonstrated in your willingness to endure in the face of all difficulties. The curious thing about persistence is that it walks hand-in-hand with self confidence. Only a person who is confident in their abilities would persist. But the more you persist, the more your belief in your abilities to achieve increases. And so it continues. An upward spiral.

LACK OF DESIRE

The atmosphere at the bobsled start is a cauldron of intensity – a blazing inferno of desire and aggression. The only times I've ever seen athletes casually stroll off the top of the hill is when an inexperienced driver is going from the top of a new track for the first time. Doing so ensures that he does not have a lot of speed, thus increasing his chances of steering the sled safely to the bottom. Once he is confident that he can negotiate the track safely, he starts off like everyone else – with intensity and maximum effort. Likewise in life, you cannot expect to leisurely stroll into a better future. There may be times when you need to tread gingerly as you learn the ropes and try to find your way, but for the most part you need to approach your goals with intense desire. The path to success and achievement must lead through desire. Desire is the burning internal quality that pushes you and creates within you uneasiness and impatience with the way things are. The great achievers, the most successful professionals, are all driven by a fire in their bellies. Regardless of the challenges they face, their burning desire allows them to transform their thoughts into action. For them, an intense, burning desire is a habit, a way of life.

LACK OF KNOWLEDGE

Knowledge is at a premium, especially in today's world where the inevitability of change dictates that those who are always learning and acquiring new knowledge will succeed the most. Now, while this is true, many individuals allow the fact that they may not have thorough knowledge of a particular subject to prevent them from launching and taking advantage of a new opportunity. Knowing that bobsledding is a winter sport is hardly enough knowledge to justify making a run at the Olympic Games, but that is exactly what we did. As the American author Ray Bradbury, whose notable works include *Fahrenheit 451* and *The Martian Chronicles*, wrote, "You've got to jump off cliffs all the time and build your wings on the way down." Mildred McAfee, an American academic who served during World War II as first director of the Women Accepted for Volunteer Emergency Service (WAVES) in the United States Navy, also chimed in on the subject. She advised: "If you have a great ambition, take as big a step as possible in the direction of fulfilling it. The step may only be a tiny one, but trust that it may be the largest one possible for now."

You do not have to know everything to start moving in the direction of your goal. You do not need to know everything about running a business to start your own. Get started with the limited knowledge you have and procure the knowledge you need as you go. Read every book, magazine and newspaper article you can about your chosen endeavor. Speak to the experts and observe how they perform. Take advantage of every chance you get to see and hear the outstanding individuals in your area of interest. Study them. Study the failures as well. Surprisingly, you will sometimes learn more from failures than you will from success.

When we were not on the track or getting ready to go on we sat on the sides watching the other athletes. At many of my speaking engagements, I am asked about the courses I have taken on public speaking. I explain that I have never taken a course, but I constantly study the subject. I am always watching speakers – motivational speakers, politicians, preachers, teachers, executives – the good, the bad, and the indifferent. By emulating successful people, you can begin your journey to success. The lessons you choose to apply will depend on your definition of success, but the more you study others, the more you become aware of what is possible in your own life, providing the motivation to push even harder.

On the run: *Another rigorous day of training in Evanston, Wyoming before going off to our pizza delivery jobs. Jason Morris is to my left and Patrick Robinson is in the rear.*

CHAPTER 10

What Stops Us from Pushing?

"Personal power is the ability to take action."
Anthony Robbins -
American Self Help - Writer and Speaker

Our personal power is like the power in a thousand pounds of TNT. The power is there, ready to explode and be a force for good or evil, but will remain latent until you choose to unleash it. Until you decide to take action you will always remain as someone with great potential for success. Envisioning the grandest of dreams and identifying the most compelling of reasons to pursue them will mean nothing if you fail to act. Through inaction you render yourself powerless and put your goals beyond your reach. Getting what you want requires that you do something. Goals and dreams are amazing creations. Desire, persistence, faith and courage are wonderful attributes, but they are not enough. Getting what **YOU** want and becoming all that **YOU** can be means that **YOU** have to take action as well. As author and motivational speaker Jim Rhon writes, "Planning, imagination and intense activity are awesome forces that have the power to dramatically change the quality of our lives. Intelligent, planned, intense and consistent activity creates new energy and keeps us moving toward the exciting future that our thoughts and desires have already created for us"

The bobsledder standing at the start is intense, focused. He has spent countless hours practicing the push and knows exactly what he needs to do to make up ground in the race or create some daylight between him and his nearest rival. He also knows that to make it happen he must actually take action. That is immediately instructive to all of us. How you feel, the skills you have developed, the knowledge you have acquired – these are but an indication of what you are capable of. In the end, the achievement of your goals is totally dependent on whether or not you took action – massive action. This is, in essence, the difference between success and failure.

There are so many examples of people who are decent, law-abiding citizens; they are highly educated, forward thinking individuals who have a genuine desire to get ahead in life. I am sure you know some of them. It might be the person sitting next to you on the train on your way to work, or in the cubicle beside yours. It could be your best friend or your neighbor. Maybe that person is you. Although you are knowledgeable, ambitious, have a great attitude and care about others, you find yourself struggling to make ends meet. On the other hand, society is filled with many semi-literate people and college drop-outs who are enjoying all the creature comforts of life. What do you suppose is the major factor that accounts for the difference?

Action!

You spend your time dreaming and talking about the promise of the future, while they invest their time in making plans and take steps to implement them. You spend your time focusing on the obstacles standing between you and your goals, while they search for solutions. You allow yourself to get caught up in the negative, discouraging things that people have to say about you, while they focus on what they need to do in order to achieve. Remember that you will always have critics. No matter how noble and altruistic or self-serving your goals are; you will always have critics, so your best option is to forge ahead.

The Jamaican Bobsled Team garnered much worldwide attention because the idea of the team seemed so novel. Even today, more than twenty years later, the phrase "Jamaica bobsled" sounds like an oxymoron. Not only did we have to deal with the fact that the concept of the team fell way outside of the accepted norms, we had deal with far more pressing, formidable challenges. We knew very little about the sport, and had even less time to gain the knowledge. The learning curve was steep. In addition, we had very little funding, substandard equipment and had to quickly learn how to make the transition from 96 degrees in the shade to living in subzero-degree weather. Needless to say, we got busy. We didn't spend time contemplating how difficult a task we had in front of us, or that many thought that we were a pack of jokers seeking media attention. We simply put our all into it and got to work. The bobsledder at the start faces enormous challenges as well, but he knows that in the end his success depends on him giving his all.

Imagine what your life would be like if you gave your all. How different would your work be if you committed yourself to spring into action? Instead of focusing on the challenges, what if you started looking for the opportunities? Rather than listen to the naysayers, imagine what you could achieve if you forged ahead towards your goals?

It is important to remember that one of the constants of life is that we are always producing results. Consider life as the currents of a flowing stream with you in it. If you just lay there, the currents will take you wherever it wishes. Through inaction, you could find yourself being thrown into jagged rocks and outcroppings and bouncing from one bank to the other all the way to the end of the stream. Whether or not those are the results you wanted, those are the ones you end up producing because you failed to take action. You just laid there as if you were powerless to affect your life experiences and ultimately the quality of your life.

On the other hand, instead of simply allowing the river to take you wherever it wishes, you could change that by looking ahead, imagining the outcome you want and, by setting goals, deliberately choose the path you want to take. Through your own efforts you avoid being caught up and carried away by the currents of your most recent crisis. Despite the challenges, setbacks, frustration, by acting – by pushing and unleashing your power – you enforce your will over your circumstances.

Taking action speaks not only to the specific steps that we need to take to achieve our goals, but also to how we actually carry our bodies. We carry our bodies a certain way depending on how we feel, and these emotional states all determine the amount of power we can unleash. Fear, doubt, anxiety, anger, joy, faith, courage, and determination all have physical manifestations. You carry your body in a specific way whenever you are experiencing any of these emotions. Have you ever noticed how your shoulders slump forward when you are depressed, how you hold your shoulders, back and chin up when you are feeling confident and courageous, or how your jaws tighten when you are angry? Your steps are strong and purposeful, your gaze steady, your handshakes firm whenever you walk confidently into a business meeting or an interview, and quite the opposite when you are afraid that things will not go your way. If you were to study the body language of the athletes at the bobsled start, you would notice that their chin is up, their shoulders are square and they have fire in their eyes. Everything about them tells you that they are operating from a position of strength. They feel ready, strong, invincible. Fear and anxiety are transformed into the powerful allies of intense focus and aggression. They are needed to overcome the resistance of the sled as they push to get up to their top speed in the first fifteen meters.

Before they step up to the start line, the athletes spend about forty-five minutes warming up by stretching as well as doing a series of wind sprints and bounding exercises. Even as they wait to step out onto the ice, you can see them jumping up and down like firecrackers just behind the starting block. They feel like they can take on the world. They feel unconquerable. They are ready.

Once again, the rituals performed by these athletes as they get ready to go down the track are instructive. Long before they got to the act of pushing the sled they had engaged their bodies physically and got themselves in a very resourceful state in order to access and unleash their power. All of us have access to the same power. I am sure that during the times when you have done something intensely physical, even though you might have felt physically exhausted deep down inside, you felt strong. Tony Robbins teaches that one of the ways you take action to unleash your power is to do an intense workout, whether it is running, biking, walking or lifting weights. Doing something in which you physically engage your body, where strength is demanded, blood is rushed through your veins, and your body becomes oxygenated will make you feel alive again. Just like the Olympic bobsledders. You will feel resourceful and invincible. You will feel like you can do anything – you can make things happen. In that state of mind, you are the bobsledder standing at the start. You will begin to take massive action – pushing against your doubts and fears, overcoming the inertia of anxiety and bursting with courage and determination. When you move into action your dreams become like a sled at the start. It first moves slowly, but as you continue to push you build up a head of steam and, before you know it, you've embarked on the ride of our life. When you move expeditiously and with a sense of urgency you unleash the power to also move your dreams from impossible to possible and from difficult to done.

PUSHING IS AN ATTITUDE

You cannot determine what the state of the economy will be, what politicians will do or what decisions your boss will make. These are but a few examples of the myriad things you have absolutely no control over. However, you have the power to chose your attitudes and hence how you will react to the circumstance of your life. One of the things that differentiate those who fail and those who succeed is that the successful ones chose a positive, empowering attitude in reacting to the challenges in their lives and the unsuccessful ones do not. A positive attitude allows you to tap into real power: certainty, confidence, courage, determination, faith, pride. A negative attitude produces disempowerment: anxiety, disappointment, doubt, fear, frustration.

Given the enormity of the challenges we faced on the road to the Olympics, it would have been easy for us to buckle under the pressure. Frankly, conventional wisdom was on our side and provided a credible way out for us, but we were possessed with a positive mental attitude, and people so possessed always feel indomitable regardless of the odds. Of course, I am not suggesting blind optimism or perpetuating some fairy tale. We know that life is not a fairy tale. As you go through life working to achieve your goals you will be confronted by very concrete facts which would suggest that you will fail. The attitude with which we choose to approach these facts will make all the difference.

Our decision to participate in the four-man event is bizarre enough to defy the Hollywood imagination. In the movie *Cool Runnings*, the script suggested that the team trained with the four-man sled from the time it was formed. The truth is that we did not start training in earnest with the four-man sled until the week of the event during the Olympic Games. At the end of the two-man competition we decided that we would compete in the four-man event so that we could all take home a medal. Call us naïve, cocky, foolhardy – whatever it is, we were already at the Olympics, so we decided to go for it. What did we have to lose? As a result, our training started full bore. The four-man is considered the premiere event in bobsledding.

It is simply a beauty to watch four hulks loading into a tiny sled as they blast off the top of the hill. Needless to say, this requires a lot more coordination and teamwork. Because of the tight spaces in which to operate, the short amount of time in which to load onto the sled, and the number of bodies involved, some interesting things can happen in the four-man event. Sometimes the two side pushers bump shoulders as they jump onto the sled, resulting in one or both of them falling off and hence a disqualification of the team. The rules state that nothing must be left on the track. So if an athlete, a cap or a push-bar falls off the sled, the team is disqualified. I have seen the brakeman, who would be the most sure-footed one on the sled, grabbing his 210-pound teammate by one hand and planting him in the sled. I have seen guys dive headfirst in the sled and, on at least two occasions, I have seen guys ride down the track backwards. One was a Russian during the Albertville Games and the other was an American. To this day, I have never been able to figure out how they did it, but such is the nature of four-man bobsledding – you do anything and everything you can to get onto the sled. We had less than a week to learn to load onto the sled without any theatrics.

With Caswell Allen declared injured and Chris Stokes replacing him, we had only a few days to teach Chris everything we knew about bobsledding; but by the end of the week we had the fastest start time.

We must move towards our goals with confident expectations. If we had faced our challenges with a different attitude in 1988, we wouldn't have succeeded to the extent that we did and our team would not have amassed any more achievements. Irrespective of the challenges you have faced, it is important to know that you have the power to overcome them. All the facts suggested that our team could not be successful in a winter sport, but our positive attitude helped us to prove them wrong. Along the way, I've learned that you should never mind the facts. I am not suggesting burying your head in the sand like an ostrich and hope that they will go away. That indeed would be foolhardy. What I know, however, is that when you focus on the solutions with a positive mental attitude you end up in a situation where you have an opportunity to create a brand new set of facts that are far more incredible, far more dynamic and far more powerful.

PUSHING IS REDEFINING YOUR LIMITATIONS

Pushing yourself to action is even harder than pushing a sled, but it is the act of pushing that gives you the greatest reward, satisfaction, confidence and personal power. You live in a world that, in many ways, is defined by limits. For example, you live within the bounds of the laws of nature. If you jump off the top of a ten-story building and flap your arms, you will not fly. You can, however, soar on the wings of your imagination as you push the envelope of what you believe is possible in your life. In pushing past your self-imposed limitations and the limitations placed on you by others you can eventually create a paradigm shift. What was impossible yesterday, through your actions, becomes today's accomplishment. Tomorrow, through your own actions, you must once again push the envelope of possibility.

I believe this to be one of the great laws of success and it is evident in every field of human endeavor. For example, in today's fast paced world of marketing and multi-million-dollar endorse-ments, it is easy to start believing that sports is only about gate receipts and winning games. What you may not realize is that sports test the limits of what the human body, mind and spirit can achieve, and that level of success can undoubtedly be dupli-cated in other areas of human effort.

In high school I ran the 800m and 1500m events. Growing up in a country generally regarded as the sprint factory of the world, I found that those were the only races I could win. Through my study of middle distance running, I became familiar with Roger Bannister and the four-minute mile. It was previously thought that man could never run the mile under four minutes. All the experts said that the four-minute mile was a physical barrier that no man could break without causing significant damage to the runner's health. They believed that the heart would explode. A man would collapse and die on the spot; the human body couldn't take it. On May 6, 1954, a little more than ten years be-fore I was born, Roger Bannister, a 25-year-old British medical student, ran the mile in 3 minutes 59.4 seconds.

Recalling the earth-shattering event more than fifty years later, Roger Bannister remarked, "There was a mystique, a be-lief that it couldn't be done, but I think it was more of a psy-chological barrier than a physical barrier." The previous record was set by Sweden's Gunder Haegg in 1945 when he ran the mile in 4 minutes 1.4 seconds. Only forty-six days after Roger accomplished the feat, John Landy of Australia lowered the new mark with a time of 3 minutes 57.9 seconds. By the end of 1957, sixteen other runners had run the mile in less than four minutes. The current world record stands at 3 minutes 43.13 seconds and more than 955 athletes have run it in under four minutes more than 4,700 times.

It is now commonplace to see not only warm weather coun-tries but also blacks competing in the Winter Olympics. Our team is still the only all-black team to have competed in the Winter Games, but bobsledding has seen teams from American Samoa, Brazil, Iraq, Mexico, Puerto Rico, Trinidad and Tobago, and the U.S. Virgin Islands. Other warm weather countries have entered the Winter Olympic as well. These include Algeria, Bermuda, Costa Rica, Greece, Honduras, Kenya, Lebanon, and Senegal. Running a sub four-minute mile and having a warm weather country competing in the Winter Olympics once seemed impossible. Today it is commonplace.

Few roads in life are easy. In fact, those leading to worthwhile goals will be strewn with challenges, obstacles and setbacks. While there will be several physical challenges that stand in your way, you don't have to be bound by them. Oftentimes our greatest triumphs lie just beyond our perceived limitations. The laws of physics dictate that human beings will never be able to fly like a bird, but by redefining our physical limitations, through gliders, airplanes and rockets, we can fly with and even beyond where birds are able.

Our biggest obstacles are always within. We are often limited by what we believe is possible. However, when we develop the courage to act on our dreams we begin the process of redefining our limits. Redefining your limits is essential for personal growth, living up to your full potential and generally improving your life. The best part of redefining your limitations is not even in the accomplishment themselves but in the sense of pride and the knowledge that you have the power to grow and adapt in order to reach higher levels of achievement.

PUSHING IS RISK TAKING

Popular beliefs say we must always play it safe. We should never burn bridges and always leave the door open. In essence, never venture out without a safety net or an escape hatch. Risk taking does not mean that you foolishly and carelessly jeopardize everything you have. It is the knowledge that new lands cannot be discovered until we lose sight of the shoreline. Bobsled athletes perform this very delicate balancing act every single time they go down the track. Once the sled is pushed over the brow of the hill there is no turning back. There are no escape hatches or safety nets, and the brakes do not work. In fact, attempting to use the brakes during the run increases your chances of crashing the sled.

The driver recognizes that he has the power to guide the sled through the many twists and turns and get everyone to the bottom of the track quickly and safely. The track offers no guarantees; however, to experience the thrill and exhilaration of riding a bobsled at 80 mph, to know what it is like to match your best against the best requires, you to face the rigors of the track.

Life is exactly like that. We have to take risks in order to improve our lives. Not taking a chance means you don't get what you want. Life offers no guarantees, but in order to smell the sweet scent of success, in order to experience the joy and satisfaction of accomplishment, and the elation that comes from knowing you grew because you stepped out of your comfort zone, you have to take risks.

There is a strong link between taking educated, calculated risks and achievement. Looking back, I realize that it took a lot of *guts* to do what we did. With only about three months to go before the Olympic Games, and with very limited knowledge, we plunged head first into learning the sport and developing our skills to the level that would allow us to compete in the Games. Theodore Roosevelt said, "Better it is to dare mighty things, to win glorious triumphs even though checkered by failure than to take ranks with those poor souls who neither suffer nor enjoy much because they dwell in the grey twilight that knows neither success nor defeat." What is it that you have not risked in your life? One thing is for sure: Those who ask very little of life because they don't want to risk failure and frustration won't be disappointed. Life will give them exactly what they asked for – very little. Whether in business, sports or life, there are no rewards without risks. However, taking calculated and measured risks allows you to unleash your power.

PUSHING IS BEING MOTIVATED

Most people think that motivation comes from an external source – an exciting event or a powerful speaker who can get them fired up. Undoubtedly external factors can provide some motivation, but that is non-sustaining. A lamp that is plugged into the wall will shine as brightly as the sun, but the minute it is unplugged the room goes dark. As long as we can stay plugged in to those external factors we will stay motivated; but since that is not practical we must find an internal source or motive. A motive is something that incites us to action. Walter Staples writes, "Motivation is a contraction of the phrase "motive-in action. It is the personification of a goal being strived for, the pursuit of something deemed desirable and worthwhile."

For all of us, the bobsled team fulfilled a long-held desire to represent Jamaica at the Olympic Games. Before the opportunity to join the team came about I was dreaming about participating in the Seoul Olympics. Every morning before reporting for duty, I would run five miles with the hope that I would be able to get in shape to compete in the 800m and 1500m events at the Games. While it was not exactly what I had in mind, being on the bobsled team gave form and flesh to my Olympic dreams and, despite the difficulties, really ignited the fire within to make it happen.

KEY POINTS TO REMEMBER - LESSON THREE

- The thirst to achieve in all areas of life comes from within and stems from the reasons why your goals are important to you. These compelling reasons are the fuel for achievement and, when mixed with action, create combustion, igniting a power in you to push past the obstacles in order to achieve your goals.

- Fuzzy goals, the inability to risk success, fear of failure and rejection, lack of belief in your ability, desire, persistence and knowledge all diminish your power and your ability to reach your full potential.

- How you feel, the skills you have developed, and the knowledge you have acquired is only an indication of what you are capable of achieving. Your success is wholly dependent on whether or not you take action-massive action.

- Pushing yourself is often difficult, but it is the act of pushing that gives you the greatest reward, satisfaction, confidence and personal power. In pushing past your self-imposed limitations – and those placed on you by others – you eventually create a paradigm shift rendering yesterday's impossibilities tomorrow's accomplishments.

- By pushing and unleashing your power, you enforce your will over your circumstances despite handicaps.

- A positive attitude allows you to tap into real power: certainty, confidence, courage, determination, faith, pride. A negative attitude produces disempowerment: anxiety, disappointment, doubt, fear, frustration.

- Focusing on the solutions with a positive mental attitude allows you to create a brand new set of facts that are far more incredible, dynamic and powerful. (continued on page 110)

KEY POINTS TO REMEMBER - LESSON 3

- Life offers no guarantees, but in order to succeed you must step out of your comfort zone – you have to take risks.

- Risk taking does not mean that we foolishly and carelessly jeopardize everything we have. Success requires taking educated, calculated risks towards achievement.

- You can unleash your power by going on an intense workout, whether it is running, biking, walking or lifting weights. By doing something in which you physically engage your body you put yourself in a resourceful state; and in that state of mind, you will feel like you can do anything. You will feel invincible.

ASSIGNMENTS

1. Get clear about your goals. Constantly remind yourself of them and then focus intensely on the rewards of achieving them.

2. Learn everything you can about your chosen endeavor. Constantly study others in your field.

3. Get on an exercise program. Do something in which you physically engage your body intensely.

See The Track Before You Take The Track

"We lift ourselves by our thought. We climb upon our vision of ourselves. If you want to enlarge your life, you must first enlarge your thought of it and of yourself. Hold the ideal of yourself as you long to be, always everywhere."

Orison Swett Marden -
American Writer and Founder of *Success Magazine*

*I*magine yourself standing at the top of a bobsled track. You are dressed warmly in a thick winter jacket and insulated pants. Your helmet firmly on, chin strap fastened, your goggles perched on top. You are standing there, chin on your chest, eyes closed, rocking from side to side, shifting your weight from one leg to the other. All around you is controlled chaos. Loudspeakers blaring intermittently, other athletes behind you going through their warm up routine, jumping rigorously, grunting, growling. Coaches shouting instructions to each other, helpers shuttling back and forth with equipment, inching the sleds closer to the start line as each sled leaves the blocks. Officials, stoic, businesslike, checking runner temperatures and ensuring that everyone is lined up in their proper order.

Over the pounding of your heart in your ear drums you can hear the deafening, almost uncontrollable screams of the crowd. Your nerves are frayed, your stomach in turmoil. You take a deep breath and exhale slowly to calm yourself down, but instead you excite the butterflies *fluttering in your stomach, sending them swirling around in a mad frenzy. The loudspeakers announce that the track is clear for you to proceed, and, as if by the flick of a switch, the crowds become silent, the butterflies are gone and your heart is now pounding with a deep sense of purpose. You turn around to check on your brakeman. No words are spoken. The fire in his eyes tells you that he is ready. You slap him on his helmet. He knows you are ready. You can hear the coach shouting "Let's go! Big push! Big push!" He is right behind the blocks but his voice seems faint, as if he is shouting at you from a mile away. You are in your own little world now. You dig your spikes into the ice, pull your goggles over your eyes, which are trained on the push bar. "Back set!" your brakeman growls. He continues, "two, three, four!" You hurl your body forward, closing your hands in a vice-like grip on the push bar, charged but relaxed, fierce but focused, muscles bulging and contracting, feet digging and churning; powering down the track as fast as you can.*

If you made a concerted effort to visualize the scene above, you no doubt would have seen in your mind's eye the white background of snow and ice, heard the screams and din of the crowds, felt the racing of your heart, the rolling of your stomach, the intensity in your body as the sled plunges down the track. If this was a little difficult for you, imagine yourself an hour late for the most important appointment of your life. Feel the frenzy with which you grabbed your pocketbook and keys and dashed out to the car. You keep asking yourself, "How could I have overslept? Why didn't the alarm go off? Of all the days this could have happened, why today?" You are weak with nervousness and anxiety. Your heart is pounding, your fingers are shaking. Traffic is flowing moderately, but hardly fast enough for you. You are darting in and out in a mad rush to get to your destination.

Or picture yourself in your favorite vacation spot. Maybe it is by the ocean, the breaking waves humming in the background. A light breeze caressing your face as you stretch out on your beach chair. Salt tingles your nose as you fill your lungs with fresh air and slowly exhale. With not a care in the world, feel the peace inside. Feel how relaxed your muscles are.

Every bobsled track has a warm house at the top. It is a staging and rest area that the athletes use before and during practice sessions and races. They are usually close enough to the start line to allow the athlete to walk only a few meters to the blocks. Two of the walls are all glass, allowing easy viewing of the start of the race and the sled sliding into the first corner. Although tinged with a bit of nervous energy, about an hour before the race starts the warm-house is an easy going, relaxed environment. During practice sessions you might even hear opposing team members cracking jokes at each other and even teasing each other about something that might have happened in the club the night before. Come race time, the atmosphere changes and the peaceful surroundings transform into a beehive.

Athletes are darting in and out, either coming in from their warm up or heading out to warm up. They are sprawled out on the floor being stretched by a teammate or massaged by the team's physiotherapist. Hovering above it all are the announcements coming over the loud speakers. Everyone passively pays attention to them, for they help you to gauge the speed at which you need to get ready – finish your stretching, put on your speed suit and ice spikes, pack your stuff and move your bag out of the way to make room for others and move your sled onto the on-deck circle.

In the midst of this mayhem, quite noticeable, are a few athletes who seem detached and almost oblivious to the tumult. They are in another world performing some tai chi-like movements. These are the drivers, and they are mentally practicing to drive the track. In their mind's eye they are seeing every part of the track. They are seeing the entrance of the curve, the middle of the curve and the line or path they want the sled to follow as they come around and see the corner *opening* up. In their minds they feel the sled react and glide off the corner as they steer the sled onto the straightway. While the spectator will only see the sled flying through the corner in a millisecond, on average the driver would have steered the sled three times. Of course, this is only possible because he visualized it beforehand. He drives the track so many times in his mind that even before he physically takes to the track the entire thing becomes something that is very familiar to him and he feels comfortable doing it. The mental rehearsals allow him to steer the sled in a Pavlovian way, almost by conditioned reflex, but probably more importantly, it gives him a sense of certainty. In his heart he knows that he can handle the challenges of the track and the race. As the author William Lyon Phelps noted, "If you develop the absolute sense of certainty that powerful beliefs provide, then you can get yourself to accomplish virtually anything, including those things that other people are certain are impossible."

Calling on the Governor General before leaving for Albertville Games, 1992.
(Left to right: *Patrick Robinson, Milton Hart, Dudley Stokes, Devon Harris, Sir Howard Cooke, Sandy Lue, Ricky McIntosh, Leo Campbell)*

CHAPTER 11

What Is Visualization?

"You must see your goals clearly and specifically
before you can set out for them.
Hold them in your mind until they become second nature."
Les Brown - Motivational Speaker

T his practice of visualization is not peculiar to bobsled drivers. All elite athletes practice it. Have you ever watched an athlete just before he or she begins a routine? Have you ever studied a weightlifter before he cleans a bar that is twice his body weight, a diver before she leaps off the platform, a basketball player at the free throw line? The image they see in those precious moments leading up to their performance often determines the outcome of the event. Known as "The Golden Goddess" of professional water skiing, Camille Duvall used mental visualization very effectively. Her unprecedented dominance of her sport for more than thirty years saw *Sports Illustrated* dubbing her as one of the "100 Greatest Female Athletes of the Century," alongside the likes of Jackie Joyner-Kersee and Nadia Comaneci. She said, "I train myself mentally with visualization. The morning of a tournament, before I put my feet on the floor, I visualize myself making perfect runs with emphasis on technique, all the way through to what my personal best is in practice. The more you work with this type of visualization, especially when you do it on a day-to-day basis, you'll actually begin to feel your muscles contracting at the appropriate times."

However, as I've demonstrated, visualization, or guided imagery, as it is sometimes called, is not reserved for athletes. Each of us has the power to visualize, and we perpetually employ this ability. Whenever you worry or get anxious about an upcoming event, you are experiencing that event through the power of your imagination. You become worried because you are visualizing an outcome that you do not want. As a result of an ingrained negative view of life many people have unconsciously imagined failure, challenges, lack, and limitation. Consequently, that is what they create in their lives.

For the most part, human beings imagine and aspire to accomplish great things in life. Great achievements begin with imagination and acting out the images you create in your mind. Athletes teach us that, through the power of our imagination, we can reach much higher levels of success. Five-time winner of the Mr. Universe title, a successful real estate mogul, blockbuster movie star and Governor of California, Arnold Schwarzenegger effectively used mental visualization to achieve at very high levels. "The mind is really so incredible. Before I won my first Mr. Universe title, I walked around the tournament like I owned it. I had won it so many times in my mind, the title was already mine. Then when I moved on to the movies I used the same technique. I visualized daily being a successful actor and earning big money."

The ability to see through the mind's eye is the most powerful, liberating endowment given to man. The mind cannot distinguish the difference between an imagined experience and a real one. It, therefore, responds to what you imagine. Through this ability you can experience an imagined event in live, vivid color, and as a result use it to achieve higher levels of effectiveness. Visualization is not some sort of self-help or metaphysical mumbo jumbo. Author Shakti Gawain describes it as, "The ability to create an idea, a mental picture, or a feeling sense of something." You can use it to perform better in your business, career, and personal life. It is important to note that, when you practice visualization, not everyone actually sees the details of an image in their minds. The athlete may actually see an orange basketball going through a hoop or a white golf ball rolling to the hole because this is a physical activity they have done hundreds of times before. But if you are using visualization to help you perform better in a meeting, you may not be able to clearly picture the physical details of the meeting because you have neither seen the people you are meeting with nor been in the room where the meeting will be held. Also, peoples' minds work differently. Some people are *eidetic visualizers*. That means that when they practice guided imagery, they see everything in bright, vivid three-dimensional color. The rest of us are noneidetic in nature. *Noneidetic visualizers* respond better to auditory, tactile, emotional, or kinesthetic cues. When you visualize, you won't necessarily see, but you will "sense" it, "feel" it or deeply think about it. So, in the illustration I just used: In preparing for the meeting, you will be able to imagine a meeting room and the general outline of the people you are meeting with, but mostly you will be sensing and feeling how relaxed and comfortable you are. You will be able to experience the confidence and ease with which you articulately express your ideas. You will be able to imagine favorable responses to those ideas.

Someone might read this and think that they can use the power of visualization to "control" the actions of others or force them to act against their will or self-interest, but that is not correct. You cannot use it to make your boss give you a raise or get your husband to take out the trash. Certainly you can imagine yourself being confident and congruent as you persuasively make your case to your boss for an increase in salary. You can imagine yourself using all your charm and guile to elicit a commitment from your husband that he will take the garbage out. In both instances, your behavior would more than likely influence how the other person responds to you. By the way, it is important to note that visualization is a tool. And like any other tool, its effectiveness is limited by the skill of the person using it. This means that everyone can improve their ability to effectively use visualization to reach higher levels of success.

The effective use of the power of visualization is a skill which can be developed and improved upon. As a novice bobsled driver, I knew that my success on the track depended not only on my ability to push the sled fast, but also on my ability to focus and create a clear picture of the track in my mind. The noises and activities in the warm house were very distracting to me and made it very difficult to focus, so I used to lock myself in a cubicle in the restroom. There, in the kind of solace that can only come from sitting on the throne, I practiced seeing and experiencing the run until my brakeman came to get me. In time, I got proficient enough to sit in my own little world in the middle of the chaos of the warm house and visualize the track.

EVERYTHING IN LIFE IS CREATED TWICE

Everything in life is created twice – first through your thoughts and then in your physical world. The clothes that you are wearing, the chair that you are sitting on, and the building that you are in right now were first created in someone's mind before they were created in reality.

Unlike animals, human beings have a free will. We can choose success or failure. We can choose to create and grow or to accept the way things are and regress. It is this ability to choose that separates us from animals. Birds fly south in the fall to warm lands, traversing thousands of miles and vast oceans; they know exactly where to go without any instruction in geography or navigation. Instinct is their only guide. Highly effective individuals train their minds to think about and visualize what they want to happen in their lives. They imagine themselves as the person they want to become. Through repeated effort they learn to control their minds and visualize their goals and dreams. The unsuccessful lack mental discipline. They allow their minds to wander from desire to desire or to become fixated on the things they do not want to have or the person they do not wish to become – and low and behold, that is exactly what they get. Each and every person, without exception and beyond a shadow of a doubt, has the ability to create what they want, since the power and potential of their imagination has no limits. The only limitations that exist are the ones you impose on your self. Few people fully understand this.

CHAPTER 12

The Weight Room Of Your Mind

"Whatever we plant in our subconscious mind and nourish with repetition and emotion will one day become a reality."
Earl Nightingale - Motivational Speaker and Author

A thletes spend a significant amount of their time in the weight room. Anyone who has worked out with weights consistently will tell you that weights strengthen and transform the body. Bobsled athletes have to be strong enough to endure the rigors of the track. The high speeds, the g-forces, the impact of the sled slamming on the walls and the pounding from a crash exact a heavy toll on the body. Weight training also helps to develop fast twitch muscle fibers that help you to be more explosive at the start. You need to cover the first fifteen meters of the track as quickly as a sprinter leaving the blocks or a running back getting through a closing hole.

Your muscles respond to the type of exercise – the intensity, the duration, the amount of weight, and the number of repetitions you do. They do not get to change any of the above, but simply respond to the work out routine. For those of you who don't work out regularly, or not at all, the muscle tone and definition that you enjoy is from the routine of your daily life. But once you go into the weight room and start working out, before long you begin to see the changes in your muscle and even experience more energy and power in your body.

Although limited by genetics, your muscles have vastly more potential for growth than you ask of them. Your mind, which has two components, the conscious and the subconscious, is the same way. In one sense your conscious mind would be like the gatekeeper of your weight room. There is no way to access all the machines and equipment in the weight room unless the gatekeeper allows you in. Your conscious mind enables you to think, process, reason logically and act on information it receives. As you are reading this, it is your conscious mind that is deciding whether or not the material is relevant to you. Your conscious mind will interpret the information and decide what is true or untrue for you and accordingly relay the information to your subconscious mind.

Once the gatekeeper allows you inside the weight room you are free to use any of the machines to perform any exercise you desire. As you know, the machines do not think. They make no judgments. They do not care how toned or flabby you are, how thin or overweight you are, or even how well you know your way around the gym; they simply perform the work you ask of them. That is how your subconscious mind works. The subconscious makes no moral judgment, cannot distinguish between what is good or bad, real or unreal, positive or negative. It has no goals to achieve except the ones you give it.

Unlike the machines in a weight room, which are limited in their capacity, the subconscious mind is limitless. Like your muscles, your subconscious mind is capable of exceedingly more than you routinely ask of it.

The muscle does not decide or even question the exercise regimen, or even the piece of equipment that will be used in the work out program; it simply goes to work based on the work-load it has been given.

You may have come across the term "muscle memory" be-fore. It describes a type of movement with which the muscles become familiar over time through repetition of a given set of motor skills. It is an unconscious process where even simple ev-eryday activities such as brushing your teeth or tying your laces become second nature. If you are an avid golfer who has been away from the course for sometime, your muscles would still "remember" how to swing the club the way you've always done it. If you decided to change your swing, your muscles would initially "resist" this new movement, but after repeated practice would accept and adapt to it. Your subconscious mind behaves in a similar way. It is the collection of memories of everything that you have ever experienced in your life – real or imagined. Every belief, conviction and thought you've ever had is based on those experiences. The same way your muscle performance is developed and strengthened through the various machines and exercises performed in the gym, psychologists maintain that your beliefs, which are supported by your subconscious mind, are formed through roughly five filters: your education, envi-ronment, past outcomes in your life, current circumstances in your life, and your creative thinking. This programming of your subconscious mind determines your habits and behaviors and ultimately your level of success. Just like your golf swing, any attempt to change the programming in your subconscious mind will meet with strong resistance. It is as if the machines in the weight room finally have a mind of their own and are refusing to let you use them. At the outset, it will take a lot of conscious effort – it will require the gatekeeper insisting that you can enter the gym and do whatever you want in order for the machines to acquiesce.

This is accomplished through visualization. The more you

practice this mental image with faith, enthusiasm and passion, the more likely you are to see it manifesting. Your subconscious mind eventually accepts these images, feelings and emotions as real; you gradually begin to believe what you imagine, and you slowly but surely act accordingly. The key to success is to control what you think about and to repeat these mental pictures until the truth reveals itself within you without a shred of doubt.

When I was growing up, I didn't know the term, "mental visualization," let alone that I was practicing it. But I used to constantly imagine myself enlisted in the officer corps of the Jamaica Defence Force after high school. Of course, it happened. While I was at Sandhurst my friend, Nick Wiltshire, would constantly talk about becoming a helicopter pilot upon his returned to Jamaica. Needless to say, he went on to become a successful helicopter pilot.

My friend Dennis Blake won a bronze medal at the 1996 Summer Olympic Games as a member of Jamaica's 1600m relay team. He told me that during his high school practices, his coach would routinely come to them posing as a reporter, holding a piece of stick in his hand for a microphone and ask. "So, Mr. Blake, how does it feel to be the 400m champion at Boy's Champs." Dennis always thought that his coach was trying to get the team to work on their public speaking skills, when, in fact, he was getting them to see themselves as champions long before the meet even took place.

CHAPTER 13

How Do You Visualize?

"I've discovered that numerous peak performers use the skill of mental rehearsal of visualization. They mentally run through important events before they happen."

Charles A. Garfield - Motivational Speaker and Author

Humans are the only beings on the planet that are aware that, as we consciously think a thought and accept it in our subconscious as true, that thought will eventually be manifested in the outer world. Without fail we all consistently act, feel and perform in concert with the dominant thoughts in our subconscious mind. Thoughts emanate from the pictures that we see in our mind's eye.

You may not realize it, but you have been subjected to years of programming. From the time you were a child you have been bombarded with thousands of messages. You have unconsciously accepted them as true, and they have guided your actions and formed your habits. Advertisers know this. That is why commercials in the media have been so effective in dictating consumer spending habits.

The mind cannot hold two conflicting thoughts at the same time. It also cannot dispel a limiting, dis-empowering belief unless you replace it with a more empowering one. Therefore, like the bobsled driver in the warm house, you have to spend time repeatedly visualizing the person you want to become and the things you want to create before your subconscious mind starts to act on it.

The following are some keys that I have adapted from my experiences on the bobsled track to the track of life.

RELAXATION

During the push start an incredible amount of energy is expended to get the sled moving. As you can well imagine, the muscles are taut and contracted as you go all out to get the sled moving. This is true for any physical activity. The harder you work physically, the quicker the work is done. The faster you chop at a piece of log with an axe, the quicker you cut through it. The same doesn't hold true in the mental realm. The harder you try to do something mentally, the more difficult it is.

On unusually cold days it takes longer for me to warm up and stretch before I get on the track. Sometimes that leaves me with less time than I would like to practice my visualization. Wanting to be at my best and feeling rushed often leads to heightened anxiety and results in me making a concerted effort to get in the *zone* and go through my visualizations. However, I have discovered that there is just no way to effectively rush the visualizations. I can't make the images I see in my mind come more quickly by making a greater effort. I can rush all the physical preparations I have to do – getting on my ice spikes, my helmet and goggles, preparing my warm bag with my extra jacket and insulated pants and sending them to the bottom of the track – but when it comes to mentally rehearsing the track, even when I was really pressed for time, I had to act as if I had all the time in the world. I achieved this by slowing down completely, closing my eyes, taking long deep breaths and letting my limbs go limp. The times when I have forced myself to see the track, I did poorly. Sometimes I even crashed.

The use of willpower to effect change through the mental realm is extremely difficult. Stop exerting so much effort on quitting smoking or some other bad habit that you are working on changing. You need to have a clear picture in your mind of yourself free of that habit before it can ever materialize. Even before you feel the urge to light up, picture yourself breaking the cigarette in two and dumping it in the trash. Of course, as we discussed before, at the outset, your subconscious mind will resist this notion because you have been conditioned, and the images of you yielding to the desire to smoke are stronger than the images of you refusing to give in. Although you will find it difficult to resist in the beginning, over time it will become easier and easier until you kick the habit. I know this might sound like hocus pocus, but this is how your mind actually works.

You can use visualization in every area of your life. Before an interview, a meeting, a confrontation, a sales presentation or any other event that you might be involved in, constantly picture it clearly, sense it, feel the emotions that you want to experience during the event until you create a sense of familiarity internally. When you eventually get to the event it will feel like you've been there before.

At the end of 1992 I began a four-year hiatus from the sport while I was adjusting to life in New York City. A few times a week, while traveling to work on the train from the Bronx to Manhattan, I would picture myself driving the track in Calgary. When I finally returned to the sport in November, 1996, instead of starting out at the half way point to slowly ease my way back in, as would have been customary, I went straight from the top of the track. It was like I had never left. Everyone was surprised, but I wasn't. I was *driving* that track every week for four years. By imagining and holding success pictures in your mind, you jumpstart a process whereby your beliefs and focus become in-extricably linked to your actions and attitudes to produce the results you are after.

SEE IT

One of the keys to good bobsled driving is to focus your eyes on the lines you want to drive because your hands will instinctively steer the sled towards that point. I learned this at the outset of my bobsled career. In an attempt to learn as much as I could about the sport, and also because I wanted to become a driver, as a brakeman I used to accompany the two drivers, Dudley and Sammy, on their track walks with the coach, Howard Siler. On those walks he would consistently emphasize the need to see the lines you want to take. "Your hands will go where your eyes are," he would often say.

As I mentioned earlier, before every speaking engagement I visualize myself on the stage. I see the audience listening to me intently as I deliver my message in a powerful, passionate way. I see myself relaxed, engaging and totally confident. I picture myself at the end of my presentation surrounded by members of the audience who have come over to thank and congratulate me for a wonderful speech. It works every time. To paraphrase our coach, your body goes where your thoughts go. Visualize success and you will achieve it. As you imagine yourself success-ful at a particular task, your conscious and subconscious minds bond to accomplish this mission.

Visualization demonstrates the mind's ability to carry out vivid images of performance – even in high pressure situations – as if they have been achieved before and are simply being re-peated. Believe it or not, as frightful as bobsledding can be, more people would prefer to go hurtling down the side of a mountain than stand in front of a room and speak to a group of people. In fact, statistics show that people fear public speaking even more than they fear death. That is because they conjure up such feelings of anxiety and trepidation that they anticipate every imaginable aspect of the process going wrong even before they take the stage. No one could possibly become an effective public speaker with such a habit.

You cannot be what you cannot see. Successful men and women have a habit of "seeing" things. They see their success in their minds long before they experience it. They picture themselves earning that promotion and winning the corner office. They see themselves completing the degree, starting their own business or starting their family. All of this imagining grooms the mind to control the body to achieve the goal. During mental rehearsals I seek to see and feel the entire run in as much vivid detail as possible. At the start, I can feel my hands tighten on the push bar. I feel the angle of my body and my legs powering over the ice as I get the sled moving. I see the first timing eye fifteen meters away. My goal is to be at top speed by the time I get there. I can feel my body flying through the air and landing softly in the sled. I hear the sled rattling underneath me; I hear the din of the crowd in the distance and feel the sway of the sled as it dances on and off the corners. Lastly, I see the lines I need to take running on top of white ice leading through the entrances and exits of the curves and I feel exhilaration as I cross the finish line. It is important to shower yourself with feelings of satisfaction just as you would if you had actually reached your goal.

The more you do this mental picturing with assurance and passion, the more likely you are to see it happen. What you are doing is literally visualizing in detail what it is that you want to take place. However, you have to repeat these mental pictures until the truth of what you are affirming resonates within you without a shred of doubt. The greater the clarity with which you visualize your goals, the more emotionally involved you are during the visualization process, and the more motivated you will be to accomplish them. The perspective from which you see your goals in your mind's eye is also important as far as the effectiveness of the practice.

THE ASSOCIATED VIEW

As we did at the beginning of this chapter, imagine that you are a bobsled driver. You have just pushed off from the start and jumped into the sled. Feel your back bracing against the seat, your feet pushing against the foot pegs, your knees jammed up against the side of the sled and your arms relaxed and resting on your legs. You can feel the sled vibrate as it picks up speed; your concentration heightens, your eyes get wider as the sled charges towards the curves. You can see the ice flashing in front of you. Feel your fingers tightening and pulling the ropes as you navigate the turns. The sled is going even faster now. It is intense as the sled whips on and off the corners. As the sled continues to accelerate on and off the corners, you can feel yourself in complete control.

The sled is going even faster now, but you are still in control; you feel your body lean to the left as your left hand gently, slowly, guides the sled off the corner and up the braking stretch. You let out an exuberant yell. As your chest heaves up and down, you realize for the first time how hard you were breathing. But it feels great. You did it!

Visualizing your goals from the associated perspective is like actually being on the sled. Not just as a brakeman in the back or a spectator watching from the side, but as the driver. You are in the driver's seat, actively participating in the accomplishment of your goals – pulling the ropes, guiding your path and experiencing all the relevant sensations. During your visualization practice, you should use this view when you want to boost the excitement, motivation and energy of your mental image by being in the game, seeing it through your own eyes.

THE DISASSOCIATED VIEW

From this perspective, you would be watching yourself through the eyes of a spectator in the crowd as opposed to seeing the run through your own eyes from the front of the sled. This would be similar to when I review my runs on a video tape.

The disassociated view is helpful for minimizing the impact of any event. The spectators at a basketball game can get very involved in the game, but they can never experience the same intensity of the emotions as the players on the court.

FREQUENCY

Even veteran drivers who have competed in the sport for many years and may have driven down a particular track hundreds of times still practice mental visualization. This is not some superstitious ritual, but a concerted effort to be successful.

Visualizing the track doesn't guarantee success. In bobsledding, as in life, nothing is guaranteed. The basketball player does not always hit the free throw, the gymnast and the diver sometimes make mistakes on their routine and the salesman sometimes loses the easy sale. Visualization, however, increases your chance of having a successful outcome a hundred fold. Throughout the day, highly effective individuals frequently imagine themselves achieving their goals. Whenever I wasn't at the track in practice sessions I would be imagining myself driving the sled. In the mornings when I woke up I would sit on the edge of the bed and visualize the corners. I would imagine that I was in the sled finding and driving the correct lines. I would do the same thing at nights before going to bed, and several times during the day.

Let's say that there was an old habit you wanted to kick to create a new positive healthier one. Several times during the day imagine, yourself practicing this new habit. Over time, a truly remarkable thing will happen: You will find yourself behaving more like the ideal person you see yourself to be. Others will also notice the change in you. Remember that you always behave in concert with the dominant images in your mind.

SAYING AND SELLING IT

The thing I disliked most in the weeks leading up to the Games in Calgary were the scores of interviews we did where we were asked about our expectations and goals for the upcoming Games. I am a firm believer in the notion that "talk is cheap." Don't tell me what you are going to do. Just do it! What I didn't realize back then was that every time I was answering that question in an interview I was selling my goals to the world and, more importantly, to myself. I supposed back then I loathed talking about them because I didn't want to be held accountable. Since then, I have found that when we tell others our goals, it holds us accountable and motivates us even more.

I am often asked which character portrayed me in the movie *Cool Runnings*. The fact is that the movie and hence the characters were all loosely based on the true story. However, if I had to choose the character that I thought was closest to me, I would have to say it was Yul Brenner; but I am also obliged to qualify my opinion. In the beginning, Yul Brenner was an angry guy who had no interest in being anyone's teammate. His only focus was to become an Olympian. I think what we saw in Yul Brenner and others like him in the world are their strong dislike of their current reality and their intense frustrations with their efforts to change it.

I believe every ambitious person who is desirous of success and believes that they have the ability to be even more successful at times find themselves dissatisfied with their progress. In that respect Yul Brenner and I are very much alike. But like me, Yul Brenner is also a dreamer. The mistake he made was that he told others about his dream. You may remember the scene where he proclaimed that after he wins the Olympics and gets famous he was going to live in Buckingham Palace. After happy-go-lucky Sanka Coffee laughed at his dream and scorned his audacity, Yul crushed the picture of Buckingham Palace he carried around to remind himself of his dreams. While encouraging Yul and defending him from Sanka's derision, Junior Bevil delivered one of my favorite lines from the movie when he admonished him to, "Go chase your palace."

I encourage you to go chase your palace; and as you do, only tell your goals and dreams to people who are like minded – the seekers. Those who set goals and pursue them with at least the same passion with which you pursue yours. Otherwise, instead of encouragement, what you will get are words of discouragement and ridicule. Some may even be chastising and derisive. Turning your dreams into reality is difficult enough as it is. You don't need those kinds of people to make it even more so.

The more important reason for telling others about your goals and dreams is what happens in our subconscious mind once you talk about them. The limitations in your minds didn't originate there. They came from an external source, primarily through your ears. We spend years hearing our parents, friends and acquaintances telling us what we can and cannot do. A child hears "no" thousands of times before she turns three years old. Through songs and commercials, the news and movies, society has programmed us for mediocrity and failure because the over riding-message through these medium has been, "I can't." As you hear yourself say your goals, you begin to believe them more and start to erode the negative programming you've been living with.

One of the keys to success is to feel in your heart that you've actually arrived even before you've started. You do that by clearly visualizing the track – seeing in your mind's eye the path that you must take, step by step. Experiencing the emotions and the sensations that the journey brings. Affirm it, believe it, commit to it and you'll finally be it.

One final word of warning. It is true; we always attract into our lives whatever we think about the most, believe in most strongly, expect on the deepest levels or imagine most vividly. However, it is important to note that these emotions and beliefs provide the internal drive for us to go pursue our hearts desire. Remember the title of the chapter; **SEE** the track before you **TAKE** the track. This implies that more and greater action is required on your part. Yes, you should visualize yourself achieving your goals, and then you have to physically go after them. You can't sit at home and visualize your goals hundreds of times and expect them to miraculously appear on your doorsteps. Visualization creates familiarity with your goals, making it easier and more likely for you to manifest them when you take action.

KEY POINTS TO REMEMBER - LESSON 4

- Each of us has the power to visualize, and we employ this ability every minute of the day. High performers use the power of their imagination to reach much higher levels of success.

- The effective use of the power of visualization is a skill which can be developed and improved upon. Effective individuals train their minds to think about and visualize what they want to happen in their lives. They imagine themselves as the person they want to become. Through repeated effort, they learn to control their minds and visualize their goals and dreams.

- The power and potential of your imagination has no limits except the ones you impose on yourself.

- Your conscious mind will interpret the information and decide what is true or untrue for you and accordingly relay the information to your subconscious.

- Your subconscious mind is incapable of distinguishing between an actual event and one that is only imagined.

- It is important to shower yourself with feelings of satisfaction just as you would if you had actually reached your goal.

ASSIGNMENT

1. Spend a few minutes everyday visualizing in vivid detail your goals and how you would like your life to be.

Courage Defeats Fear

"All life is a chance. So take it!
The person who goes furthest is the one
who is willing to do and dare."
Dale Carnegie - American Writer and Lecturer

In the movie *Cool Runnings*, there is a scene depicting a roomful of potential bobsledders watching some old footage of bobsled crashes. The grainy, black and white images of jaw-dropping, eye-popping crashes left everyone squirming in their seats. It was a shocking introduction to a sport where, as John Candy's character puts it, "You don't break bones; you just get them crushed." The empty room at the end of the viewing never fails to solicit a few laughs. The humor was belied by a very significant truth: They all ran away because they were afraid.

In real life, there were about forty of us viewing the clips in a small room on one of the upper floors at the National Stadium in Kingston. The footage they showed that day was far more horrific than was seen in the movie. Of course, there were the usual crashes where the sleds flipped upside down with the athlete's head dragging on the ice. But then there were some spectacular ones as well. There were crashes in which the sleds flew out of the track and crashed into the trees. Reminiscent of the footage on ABC's *Wide World of Sports* of the skier flying off the course, crashing through the barriers and into the crowds, there were a few clips in which the athletes were thrown from the sleds, skidded over the edge of the track and ended up in the crowd of bystanders. However, the crash that stands out in my mind was one that was depicted in a still shot. The crash took place during the 1981 World Championships in Cortina D'ampezzo, Italy. In the photo, I saw four bodies strewn along the track, there was blood everywhere and the driver looked as if he was decapitated. I later discovered that the driver was James "Nitro" Morgan. His brother, John, a former bobsledder as well, was serving as a color commentator for the race in which Jimmy (as James was often called) lost his life. They were natives of Saranac Lake, NY. Jimmy represented the United States in the 1976 Winter Olympic Games in Innsbruck, Austria, where he finished in 14th Place in the two-man event and 15th in the four-man event. Several years later John told me about his brother's love for life and the sport he died doing. I also learned that he wasn't decapitated; when his sled tipped over, his neck slammed on the wall causing a gaping wound, and in the process he broke his neck. His crew walked away from the crash, shook up but alive. Ironically, Jimmy Morgan's death, coupled with the death of stuntman Paolo Rigon a week later on the same track during the filming of the James Bond movie *For Your Eyes Only*, prompted officials to shorten the track from 1,720m to its current distance of 1,350m.

We were also shown another fatal crash that day. This one took place in Lake Placid, NY. Sergio Zardini was an accomplished Italian bobsled driver. In 1964, the year I was born, he won a silver medal at the IX Olympic Winter Games in Innsbruck, Austria. Between 1958 and 1962, he won a total of ten medals at the The Federation Internationale de Bobsleigh et de Tobogganing (FIBT) World Championships. He migrated to

Canada after the 1964 Olympics where he continued to compete as a member of the Canadian team. The crash we saw on the footage took place in February 1966. He was the reigning World Champion at the time.

Tony Carlino, who competed on the American team between 1975 and 1988, was there and filled in some of the details for me. Zardini had the fastest time in the heat before and was charging at almost 90 mph towards Zig Zag. Zig Zag was a double curve. It got its name because it slammed the sleds into a really sharp left hand turn and then back to the right. Zardini's sled flew through zig correctly but he lost control of it as it roared into zag. The sled flipped on its left side violently and slid and scraped along the wall of zag. As the sled went around the curve, it slammed into the lip – the wooden overhang that is built onto the curves to prevent the sleds from flying out of the track. The lip on Zig Zag was put in place after the 1932 Olympics, during which two German sleds shot off the course. Even so, many drivers disliked it, and one American driver withdrew from the race after another sled crashed there before Zardini. Unfortunately, the highest point of the sled was Zardini's head, which was protected with only a leather helmet. The impact tore his helmet off, leaving his face and skull totally exposed. As they skated down the track, Zardini's head was literally planed by the rough wood. Mike Younger, his teammate sitting behind him, also rammed into the lip. The force of the impact snatched both men from the sled, which continued down the track with the remaining two crewmen. The bodies of the two ejected men eventually came to a stop, Zardini leaving a trail of blood behind. Younger, who was unconscious, sustained relatively minor injuries; but Zardini was decapitated.

As I watched the footage that warm, sunny afternoon in Kingston, I felt a chill up my spine. There was a huge lump in my throat as I sat there, ash-faced, wondering what I was getting myself into. The room was quiet, almost somber. After such a jarring introduction to the wonderful world of bobsledding, the following day about half the group failed to return for the rest of the trials. Like the potential bobsledders in *Cool Runnings*, they were gripped by fear.

Roughly one month after viewing those clips, I rode in a sled for the first time. In mid October, 1987, our team went to Calgary to begin our crash-course ice training for the Games. I had never seen before so much ice and cold – enough to build whole platoons of snowmen – and it turned out to be a whirlwind introduction to a sport we were expected to master in a few short months. One of the first orders of business in Calgary was to do a track walk. The purpose of the track walk is two fold: It allows the driver to study the ice, especially at the entrances and exits to the corners. It would be important for him to know if there was any ice build-up in those areas overnight or if the track crew did any excess shaving of the ice. The track walk, which lasts between thirty and forty-five minutes, also allows the driver to mentally prepare by visualizing each turn as he studies them. We learned that the driver always walks the track before practice and races. The one thing that I found odd about the track walk was the fact that they started at the bottom of the track and worked their way up. You would think that they would walk the track in the direction that they would be sliding – from top to bottom. I was told that the track walk is done from bottom to top because it saves time. Later, after I had become a driver, I started doing my track walks starting from the top. I was convinced that it would be more sagacious to walk the track in the direction I would be racing. I soon discovered that the usual way actually made more sense. When you do your walk from the bottom to top, you find yourself at the top of the track at the end of your walk. This gives the driver ample time to make some last cursory checks of the sled and relax before he has to start his warm ups. Perhaps more importantly, it does not diminish, in any way whatsoever, his ability to study the corners and to visualize them in the correct order. If he is at the bottom of the track then he has to wait for a ride back to the top, and that eats up his time. Being brand new to the sport, our coach invited the brakemen on the track walk as well. The track was an ominous sight. The corners seemed really tall and the space between the end of the corners and the beginning of the straight ways seemed so narrow. It was difficult for me to imagine how anyone could safely and successfully navigate them.

At the end of the track walk came the fateful moment. It was actually time to go down the track. It was bobsled time. The butterflies that began swirling around in my stomach ever since I arrived in Calgary were now in a frenzy. Samuel Clayton was my driver. He had never driven a sled before, and yet I was climbing in one behind him. It might be hard to believe that someone coming from the tropical sunshine of Jamaica could have sweaty palms in sub-zero degree weather, but I am pretty sure I did. I was weak with nervousness. To be perfectly honest, I was close to wetting myself. As I sat down and braced myself in the sled, I began to get flash-backs of all those horrible crashes I had seen in Jamaica. I had never quite got the image of Zardini's and Morgan's lifeless bodies sprawled on the ice out of my head, and now they were foremost in my mind.

During the track walk our coach, Howard Siler, and Joey Kilburn, who was with the Canadian Junior team, took great pains to point out to us that the sleds can't fly out the tracks anymore. The wooden lips on the top of the curves keep them in the track. I had seen the lips, but I had also seen the rainbow of colors that helmets have left on them because the sleds went too high on the corners. It was reassuring that I wasn't going to take a bobsled flight, but I also knew that Sergio Zardini and Jimmy Morgan didn't fly out of the track. They were lying right there on the ice, blood everywhere. I had cotton throat, my knees wobbled under me, my heart pounded and I'm sure my blood pressure soared. I donned my helmet. My breath caught in my throat as I choked. I loosened it, but it was too slack – not safe. I tightened it again and uneasily took my place behind Sammy. "Ready, fellows?" Joey Kilburn asked. He was holding on to the back of the sled so that we could climb in. I kept trying to picture myself in one piece, hoping that this would help me through the ordeal. By now I was an absolute wreck with nervousness. I pulled my goggles down. "If I die, I die; but here we go," I thought.

Joey nudged us off and then, as the sled picked up momentum, held on to it to slow it down as much as possible. My heart hammered in my ears. My fingers tightened around the handlebars, and I leaned forward and rounded my shoulders in order to jam them against the sides of the sled, while stiffening my legs and bracing my knees outwards to wedge myself in. Because we were brand new in the sport, we didn't start at the top of the track. As is customary, beginners start at the halfway point on the track – the *Damen* start. Damen means "lady," reflecting the German influence on the sport. We crawled around the bottom of corner six and then trickled into seven – a long left hand turn; off seven into turn eight on the right and down the long straight way, the fastest part of the course. The wind was whistling over the drumbeat in my ears. Corner nine is a 270-degree turn called the *kriesel* – the German word for "circle." As we charged through nine, I could feel the g-forces pushing me down into the sled. Although I could see nothing but flashes of white, I strained to hold my head up. Out of *kriesel* into ten. By now our speed rocketed. Although we were probably going no faster than thirty miles per hour, it felt like we were flying. The extra speed pushed us up higher on the curves. As we slid into eleven, the sled got high onto the turn and tilted to one side. I worried that we would tumble, but we didn't. Twelve on the right. Thirteen on the left, and then a long fourteen on the right. I exhaled. "Thank God," I prayed.

I have never doubted that I would be able to be a world class bobsledder. Sure, it has been challenging, and there have been some frustrating moments, but I've always believed I had the ability to succeed. My biggest challenge has always been fear. People have always looked at me with disbelief or think I am pulling their legs when I tell them that I am scared of speed and height. I was recently invited to Calgary to commemorate the twentieth anniversary of their hosting of the Olympics. The ski jump at the Canada Olympic Park no longer meets the specifications to be used in international competitions, and since it would be far too costly to demolish and rebuild, the thing is now used as a zip line. It is reputed to be the tallest one in North America. Michael Edwards, better known as "Eddie the Eagle," was also invited to the event and agreed to do the zip line for the benefit of the press. Someone came up with the bright idea that I should do the zip line with Eddie and, for reasons that still confound me, I agreed to do it. We decided to do a practice jump the evening before the event. When we got to the tower we discovered that the elevator was broken. Our next option was to walk up the five stories by stairs, which was just fine with me until someone suggested that we should use the outside stairs. Eddie and the others were bounding up the stairs ahead of me and engaged in a lively conversation while I was in the back holding on as tightly as I could to the railing, gasping and hyperventilating. I had to jump from five stories above Calgary. Twice. One practice jump, and one for the press. I was scared to death, but I did it. Why? You wonder. Why would I do something that scares me so much? How could I be so passionate about bobsledding when it scares me so much? The answer is simple. Every time I go down the track it represents another occasion that I have taken on and conquered my fears. When you accept your fears and act despite those fears, you conquer them. As Mark Twain reminds us "Do the thing you fear and the death of fear is certain."

A visit to the Soosobana Elementary school in Nagano, Japan, 1998.

CHAPTER 14

What Is Fear?

"Fear is nature's warning signal to get busy."
Henry Link - American Psychologist

The air we breathe is filled with oxygen which sustains life. It also contains carbon dioxide which, as you know, does not support life but is always in our bodies. Our body ensures that the carbon dioxide doesn't build up to levels that would inhibit our ability to function or, at worse, kill us. In the same way that all of us have some carbon dioxide in our bodies, there is no such thing as a person without fear. You may be surprised to learn that the fear of falling and the fear of loud noises are the only two fears that most children are born with, and experts believe that even those fears may have been acquired in the womb. It appears that all the other fears that we have were learned. Some may even argue that many of our fears are inherited from our forefathers – early man, who lived with a heightened sense of awareness so as not to become dinner for some predator.

The bottom line is that we all have fears of one kind or another, and it is nothing to be ashamed about. It is a natural part of everyday life, and the extent to which we succeed or fail is determined by how we react to and deal with our fears.

There are many legitimate, healthy fears that serve us well. You should have a healthy fear of putting your bare hands on a hot stove or leaning over the balcony several stories above the ground. In New York City, where I live, you should definitely have a healthy fear of stepping off the curb without first checking to see if there's a yellow cab in the vicinity.

These are realistic fears that are desirable and sensible to have. They keep us safe and alive, the same way they protected our ancestors centuries ago. The key to dealing with our fears is to not allow them to take charge of our lives through neglect or avoidance. We must learn to manage them, and by doing so we empower ourselves to do the things we need to do to succeed. You conquer your fears by taking action. We will delve into this later, but know that in order to take action we have to learn the rules. In the examples cited above, we learn very quickly how to navigate around a hot stove after we've been burnt the first time, and it is certainly foolhardy to sit at home refusing to go out on the streets because we might get hit by a car. We simply learn and apply the rules of traffic. Fear of losing their principal have kept many people out of the stock market, and thus prevented them from having their money work as hard for them as they have worked for it. Of course, there is always an inherent risk, but guided by a healthy fear and learning the rules of traffic, investing, or the laws of physics we are able to cross the streets, invest in the stock market, cook a meal or do any other number of things that involve risks.

The fear that the other potential bobsledders and I felt on that warm, sunny afternoon watching footage of bobsled crashes was legitimate. The strong possibility that we could get killed or seriously maimed on a bobsled track far from the lush green hills overlooking Kingston was real. In 1989, the year I learned to drive bobsleds, two young Eastern European drivers were killed, and I am aware of others who have been killed or, as in the case of my friends Joe Sisson and Travis Bell on the American team, have sustained serious, debilitating injuries. I have sat wide-eyed as Lenny Paul, a brakeman from Great Britain, told us of the horror he felt when his driver's lifeless body fell backwards on his lap during a crash at Lake Placid. All the blood convinced Lenny that Mark Tout was decapitated, but thankfully it was only a deep gash on his skull. What separated the twenty or so of us who turned up for the trials from the ones who didn't was how we each handled our fears. Those of us who completed the trials decided that we would not be controlled by fear; that instead we would control it. Although the decision was not a conscious one, the fact that we turned up for the trials was the first step in controlling our fears. We took action. And for those of us who were selected to the team, the second thing we did was to learn how to control the bobsled safely, and thus reduce the risk of serious injury.

Fear is one of the biggest obstacles to success. Subconsciously, we allow fear to convince us that we are unworthy, undeserving, inadequate or incapable. Fear points it out, and we begin to believe that we lack the right skills, level of education and experience. It highlights the fact that we were born on the wrong side of the track, the wrong family or the wrong social pedigree.

The more we believe in these lies, the more food and energy we feed to this monster lurking in the closets of our mind – an exercise which is debilitating mentally, emotionally, even physically. It prevents us from discovering our talents and keeps us trapped in our comfort zone. It emphasizes the obstacles instead of uncovering the possibilities. It highlights the pitfalls, darkening the ray of hope in our lives instead of showcasing the rewards and affirming the benefits.

I have often heard it said that **FEAR** is an acronym which means **F**alse **E**vidence **A**ppearing **R**eal. In other words, the fears that we have are baseless. They are a figment of our imagination. However, we embrace them. They are emblazoned on our mental disks and replayed so often they have become the tunes we dance to every time we set out to do something great. Many of us are failing to explore our full potential because fear cripples us. What lies have you been conjuring up and listening to? What fears are influencing and controlling your behavior to the point that they are preventing you from living the life of your dreams? As Rudyard Kipling stated, "Of all the liars in the world, sometimes the worst are your own fears"

FEAR WALKS WITH CHANGE

Growth and success are born of change. Success, however you may define it, requires that you grow in a particular area of your life so that you can accomplish something you have never done before. To grow means that you are changing. If you are learning a new skill or dropping an old habit, it means that you are changing and growing at the same time.

Starting a new business venture, switching careers, getting married – putting yourself out there in any way – are all things that represent significant changes in your life. They also represent great uncertainties. No one can tell for sure how things will turn out. Statistics claim that 1 in 5 new businesses close their doors during the first 3 years, and 50% of marriages end in divorce. The uncertainty that accompanies change gives rise to fear. Equally powerful is our resistance to change. Many people are content with the status quo. They are at a loathe to venture from the comfortable, convenient confines of their ordered lives. They've contended that a tight grasp on the reins of life is the best way to go. But alas, that is not the path to success.

"Nothing ventured; nothing gained."

"Success is a journey not a destination."

These well used clichés support the view that we, in our quest to live up to our full potential, must embrace the idea of change. That's what successful people do. Successful individuals – whether they are executives, students, craftsmen, nurses – are those who are constantly learning and developing new skills. They commit themselves to change so that they can grow, get better and become more successful. They have to contend with uncertainties and the possibilities of failure. Like everyone else, these high performers experience the emotion of fear, but they do not allow it to get in the way.

WHAT IF?

The not-so-successful are always preoccupied with what could go wrong. This way of thinking dictates that they must have all the facts and all their ducks lined up in a row before they set a new venture in motion. The question "what if?" dominates their thinking. At first blush this seems like a reasonable, legitimate question for anyone to ask. There is nothing wrong with looking on the downside of any action we are undertaking. In fact, it is prudent to do so, and to make contingencies just in case things do not go as planned. However, in the case of the low performers this question and way of thinking is really a façade for their fears: Their fear of change. Their fear of failing. Their fear of looking foolish in front of their peers. Their fear of rejection. They invest so much time pondering what could go wrong and preparing for any eventuality that they never get started.

It goes without saying that detailed planning is essential for success, but high performers know that if they wait to have every little thing perfect then they would never get started. As author and publisher William Feather reminds us, "Conditions are never just right. People who delay action until all factors are favorable are the kind who do nothing." High performers dream, set goals, create plans and consider contingencies but never allow the fear of what might go wrong to prevent them from getting started. They expect and accept that things will not always go as planned, and are always armed with their creative powers to find a way around the inevitable obstacles.

In keeping your fear in its place, you must focus more on the goal and less on what could go wrong. In bobsledding, the novice is always coached on what to do in the event of a crash; however, the bulk of his instruction is on how to get to the bottom of the track quickly and safely. If you have ever traveled by airplane, you are well aware that as you taxi down the runway the flight attendants go through the safety briefing while the pilots are focused on the take off. Time is spent considering the contingencies, but the major focus is on what needs to be done to successfully complete the journey. Successfully navigating the path to your goals requires that you consider what could go wrong; work out your plan of action and then work towards your goal as if everything will fall perfectly in place.

When we start to dwell on the possible negative results and our thoughts become dominated by the *what ifs*, we lose focus of the intended goal. I have seen more than a few proven, exceptional athletes let their fear of crashing prevent them from even becoming mediocre bobsledders, let alone the world class sledders they could have been. I am sure you know of at least one person who refuses to fly. All they can think about is the possibility of crashing. *What ifs* provide a healthy, nutritious diet for our fears, and these are born out of a discomfort with the unknown and a lack of faith in our abilities. Because of these two factors, we begin to imagine all the things that could go wrong with the venture we are undertaking. As it turns out, the more we ponder what could go wrong, the more clearly those images are emblazoned in our mind. Since your dominant thoughts eventually manifest themselves, your fears eventually become your reality. Remember Job in the Bible? He woke up everyday worrying about losing his possessions and eventually it happened. He was left lamenting, "My worst fears have come true."

Trading in my bobsled uniform for my Army uniform.

CHAPTER 15

What's the Absolute Worst That Could Happen to You?

"My life has been full of terrible misfortunes most of which never happened."
Michel de Montaigne - French Renaissance Writer

My fear of speed and height made bobsledding a challenging proposition for me. This became even truer when I turned my hand to driving. I really wanted to do well, but I also knew that any progress I could possibly make was being impeded by my fears. One day I read a story about a master on the tight rope who was teaching his young student. The student was tentative and afraid. Like me, his fears were standing in the way of his progress. The master told him to visualize himself falling off the high wire. The apprentice did and discovered that not only could he survive a fall, but the worst of it was in his imagination. He went on to become a master tightrope walker himself. After reading this story, I started picturing myself, before every run as I waited for the track to be cleared, rolled up in a ball, rolling down the track at high speeds, ricocheting off the walls.

That imagined experience was far worse than any crash I had experienced (and I had experienced quite a few) and so I was able to eventually put my fears in check. The worst of it was in my mind. The truth is that crashing a bobsled isn't always as bad as it looks on television. Our crash in the four-man event is one of the most spectacular ones I've ever seen. You can't help but cringe when you see the sled go airborne and our heads slam against the hard ice going seventy-five miles an hour. To see the violent way in which the sled whipped around the corners as we skated down on our heads, and Dudley Stokes' neck wedged between the sled and the wall of ice as we came around the final bend, definitely gives you cause to pause. However, as someone who was on the sled, I have to say that it was not half as bad as it looked. You might find it surprising to learn that more people are injured off the track than are injured on it. It is a little like air travel. When a plane crashes, people are horrified by the number of deaths, yet more people die in car crashes annually than in airplane crashes. It is routine for athletes to slip and fall on the ice, pull a hamstring or sustain some other form of injury. I have seen an athlete from Eastern Europe scream in agony as blood dripped from his crushed fingers. His teammate tried to take a short cut when moving the sled around and that ended his season. Crashing represents a failure. It occurs because of a lapse in concentration or an inability to perform a delicate maneuver to negotiate the turn. Both of these can be remedied through repeated practice. Above all, though, these failures represent an opportunity for us to learn and get better.

I think it was wise to show the crash footage at our team trials. The chance to compete in the Olympics was undoubtedly alluring, but it was also important for us to know that the path to the glimmer and glamour of the Olympic Games was a difficult and dangerous one. I believe that assessing the worst thing that can happen to you as you attempt to conquer your fear is somewhat liberating. There is no science to this, though – this is a very personal process. You may determine the worst thing that could happen will more than likely not happen, and that gives you the courage to go on. On the other hand, if you are unwilling to accept the worst thing that could happen if it did in fact occur, then you should find another goal to pursue. So, what is the worse that could happen to you? Bankruptcy, criticism, embarrassment, exhaustion, humiliation, injury, rejection, ridicule? Let's say you were presented with the prospect of pursuing a new business venture. You would no doubt be excited about the possibilities, but at the same time you might find yourself consumed with fear about losing all your money and possibly going bankrupt. If you can live with the fact that you might go bankrupt, then you stand a good chance of success; but if the prospect of being bankrupt is unpalatable to you, then you shouldn't try launching a new business.

In pursuing my desire to become an Olympic bobsledder, I realized that the worst thing that could happen to me is that I could literally lose my head in the effort. I realized, though, that the chances of that happening were very slim. Crashing a sled is a little like an umpire getting hit by a pitch in a baseball game. It can happen, and when it does, no one is shocked and the umpire is usually able to laugh it off and continue with the game. The vast majority of the time, we walk away from a bobsled crash with nothing more than a bruised ego.

I have been known to half jokingly say that we wear helmets to make sure we do not get killed. In other words, we take precautions to minimize the risks and then go for it. Full out. We do not tiptoe off the top of the hill. Win, lose or draw, we put every ounce of energy we have into the push, and take the challenge of the track and our fears head on. Stop avoiding failure and criticism. You may have to risk bankruptcy in order to become a successful entrepreneur. There can be no success without the risk of failure. No acceptance without the risk of rejection. Fear is a negative emotional response to risk. It is imagining a negative outcome because of the risks we have to take. There are always risks in life. Nothing in life is certain, but if you want to improve your life, you have to be prepared to take risks.

Jamaica finished 8ᵗʰ nation overall in the four-man event in Lillehammer, 1994.

CHAPTER 16

What Is Courage?

"Courage is being scared to death... and saddling up anyway."
John Wayne - American Film Actor

Ask any one familiar with the sport and they will tell that, in order to be a good bobsledder, you need to have strength, explosive speed and power, and the driver needs to have good hand-eye coordination. All of this is true, of course, but if you were to ask me I would say that there is one overarching quality, a quality that no coach can teach, but one that is absolutely necessary to be a world class bobsledder – courage. In 1991 we invited one of the athletes from the Summer Olympic team to join our team. This guy was no tortoise. He had won a silver medal as a member of Jamaica's 4 x 100m relay team in the Seoul Olympics, but he didn't even last a week with us. Before every run he donned more padding than a football player, his eyes were bigger than my bulging fists, and he ran like a ballerina tip-toeing around the dance floor. He lacked the level of courage needed to be successful in the sport.

In our society courage is synonymous with heroes. A soldier

in battle, a fireman rushing into a burning building or someone diving after a drowning person in the swelling ocean all conjure up images of courage. This is what would be described as physical courage – the ability to face physical pain, hardship, or threat of death.

However, courage has another side as well. It can be seen in the kid who stands up to a schoolyard bully, the salesperson who picks up that 2-ton telephone to set up appointments or the woman who leaves her secure job with benefits to start a business doing something she really loves. The person who blows the whistle on corporate corruption or the teenager who resists peer pressure to drink, smoke, or use drugs are also exhibiting courage – moral courage, the ability to act rightly.

The two things that are common to all these scenarios are fear and action. They represent legitimate fears – being involved in a firefight or a daring rescue at sea would give anyone cause for concern. On the other hand, confronting someone, quitting a good job or saying "no" to your friends is hardly life threatening. However, all of these scenarios demonstrate a fair amount of uncertainty in the outcomes, and this leads to you feeling afraid, anxious, apprehensive, or scared.

The emotion of fear is always swirling just below the surface, lying in wait, looking for the right opportunity to attack your mind – and the only way to defeat it is by taking action. The soldier, the firefighter, the kid on the playground, the woman leaving her job, the teenager resisting peer pressure; they all felt fear but acted in spite of it. That is what you call courage. Many believe that to be courageous means to be fearless, but that is not so. The World War I fighter ace and Medal of Honor recipient Eddie Rickenbacker once said, "Courage is doing what you're afraid to do. There can be no courage unless you're scared." Fear exists in everyone and comes up every time you move forward on your journey from where you are to where you want to be.

Successful people are courageous not because they have no fear but because they felt the fear and pursued their dreams anyway.

Whenever a bobsledder pushes that sled over the brow of the hill and jumps in, any number of unpleasant events can play out. He is aware of them, but chooses to focus only on the positive and on what he is trying to achieve. In one courageous act, he pushes the sled as hard as he can and goes charging down the track. Face your fears in this manner enough times and in time it begins to lose its grip on you. As Eleanor Roosevelt said, "You gain strength, courage, and confidence by every experience in which you really stop to look fear in the face. You must do the thing which you think you cannot do."

Courage is the antidote for the poison called fear. When you act courageously in one area of your life you will be more inclined to act courageously in other areas of your life as well. So be courageous. Act. As the Nike commercials say, "Just do it!" Do it and you will find that instead of being paralyzed and held down by fear you will be emboldened and invigorated with excitement and enthusiasm, and in that state of mind you will feel powerful and unstoppable. You were afraid, but you still did what you feared most. If fear is the enemy of success, courage is its great ally. If fear blocks you from reaching your full potential, courage is the conduit to an abundance mentality and a life of limitless potential.

STEP OUT IN FAITH

A twelve-year study of successful entrepreneurs conducted by Babson College concluded that the only thing they had in common was the willingness to launch, to step out in faith, to act without any guarantee of success. Once they had started, they learned the lessons they needed to succeed. Daring, boldness, audacity, faith – these are all words that can be associated with the Jamaican bobsled team and all are integral components of courage.

For many around the world, the United States of America represents an opportunity to pursue their dreams and live the life they've always imagined. As an immigrant, I am intimately familiar with the enormous amount of courage it takes to uproot yourself from the security of everything you know and are familiar with to move to a strange new culture armed with nothing more than hopes and dreams. There is a saying that is perhaps common to every army in the world. Army life is good because we get, "three meals a day, have no bills to pay and no wife to obey." This speaks to the sense of job security that we all get from serving in the military. Growing up, I had decided that if I could somehow make it to the Officer Corps of the Jamaica Defense Force, I would be happier than a pig in slop. But here I was, eight years after reaching that milestone, getting ready to walk away from it. I remember one of my friends asking how I was able to muster the courage to leave. My response was simple: "It was an act of faith."

Our team dared to attempt a sport that was not just alien to us, but one that we only had the most basic of knowledge of. We were bold enough to face the enormous challenges that came with such a seemingly impossible undertaking. We had the audacity to think that we could actually become very good at this in such a short space of time; and because we had faith that somehow it would all come together, we threw ourselves into it without reservation.

Throughout the ages, every great discovery, every great accomplishment or adventure that man has embarked on began this way. They had the temerity to step into the vast unknown. They had the courage to dare, to boldly go where no man had gone before. Look back in your life. Recall your proudest, greatest achievement. Was it handed to you on a silver platter, or did you have to strive and struggle? Were you guaranteed success before you started, or did you simply forge ahead with confident expectation? Was your path safe, or did you have to throw caution to the wind and risk it all? Were you hindered by fear, or did you just launch in faith? Dr. Joan L. Curcio, the first female professor in Educational Administration at Virginia Tech, reminds us that "Courageous risks are life-giving, they help you grow, make you brave, and better than you think you are."

It takes courage to strike when the iron is hot. To go after your dreams even when those you love the most don't believe in them and would rather you fulfill the vision they have for your life. In *Cool Runnings*, Junior Bevil's burning ambition was to become an Olympian. His father, who also understood what it took to be successful, envisioned his son as a lawyer in a Miami firm. Luckily for Junior, as difficult and nerve wracking as it was, he had the courage to go against his father's wishes and listen to his true self.

To qualify for the 1988 Olympics meant getting sponsorships, purchasing a sled and other related equipment, and investing time to learn and master a brand new sport. Conventional wisdom dictated that this was an impossible task, and even if we could somehow pull it off, it would take years. We did it in months. Conventional wisdom, it seems, is over rated at times. How many times have you taken the counsel of your fears and paid homage to conventional wisdom? What has been done in the past, other people's beliefs and your environment on the whole, if allowed, can limit what is possible in your life. It takes courage to ignore conventional wisdom in order to sail across the high seas of possibilities.

TAKE ACTION

It is true that the importance of learning, understanding and practicing cannot be overlooked. Likewise, a risk-benefit analysis should be part of the process. However, the real value of something can only be proven after it has been tried and tested.

Don't spend half of your life in school getting educated and developing new skills – get out in the real world. Don't take forever researching and developing your new idea – take it to the market.

Take Action!

As a novice bobsled driver, I realized that all the theory in the world was useless to me until I faced my fears and took to the track. Once on the track I had to have faith in my ability to drive the sled. Anyone with a basic knowledge of bobsledding knows that the brakes are only applied at the end of the race, on the part of the track known as the braking stretch. Once the sled goes over the brow of the hill and gathers momentum, there is no viable way to stop it. If the brakeman was to slam on the brakes during a run, he would succeed in making the track workers and the other teams livid, slow the sled down slightly and cause the driver to lose control. Knowing this, my intention was to navigate every run successfully, and my definition of success constantly changed. Initially, a successful run simply meant getting to the bottom of the track upright on all four runners. Then it meant getting down without hitting the walls and shaving hundredths of a second off the time. With every corner I drove, with every run I took, I was improving my skills, redefining my limits and pushing back the fear. There was no time to think about slamming on the brakes. I was in control.

If you truly want to live a life without limits, you've got to act. You've got to get on the track, take your foot off the brakes and go. As you navigate the twists and turns, you will learn and grow and your skills will improve. As your skills improve, your confidence grows, and as your confidence grows so does your faith in your ability to reach your goals. Fear dissipates in the face of faith and confidence, but it all starts with action.

General Douglas MacArthur said, "There is no security in life, only opportunity." Life offers no assurances, but it is abundant with possibilities. When we act despite the false evidence that tells us those possibilities don't exist, we begin to uncover what is possible. Your lack of courage is costing you more than you will ever know. I was able to take advantage of an incredible opportunity because I had the courage to chase my dream of being an Olympian.

Being Jamaican, as you can imagine, I like reggae music. You might be surprised, however, to learn that I also like country music. A lot. I suppose it must be amusing to see a Jamaican bobsledder driving around New York City listening to country music. One of my favorite songs is "I Hope You Dance," by Lee-ann Womack. What she is saying in the song is that when life presents opportunities, you should take advantage of them. Do not sit on the sidelines as life's music is playing – Dance! Take action! Make the first step! Do it! Do something. Anything. It doesn't matter what action you take as long as you move in the direction of your goals, even while you are still feeling fearful.

If fear is holding you back or preventing you from enjoying your life to the fullest, it's time to take action. Think of all the things you have robbed yourself of, the contributions you could have made, the people who you could have inspired, the things you could have provided for your family, if only had you pushed past your fears.

An old English proverb reminds us, "a faint heart never won fair lady." Human beings are built for courageous living. Act even when you are afraid, because courage is the conduit that leads us from the paralysis of fear to the rewards and possibilities of the unknown.

KEY POINTS TO REMEMBER - LESSON 5

- Fear is a natural part of everyday life and everyone has fear of one kind or another.

- Some of your fears are legitimate, but most are baseless figments of your imagination. They are **F**alse **E**vidence **A**ppearing **R**eal.

- Fear is one of the biggest obstacles to success. The extent to which you succeed or fail is determined by how you react to and deal with your fears.

- Courage does not mean the absence of fear, but rather that you take action towards achieving your goals even though you might still feel fearful.

- When you do the thing you fear, it eventually loses its power over you.

- One courageous act in one area of your life will have an incredibly powerful effect in all the other areas.

ASSIGNMENTS

1. Acknowledge that you are creating your fear and identify the ways in which it is holding you back.

2. Outline the pay-off for eliminating this fear. Pause, reflect, practice deep breathing and imagine all the benefits you would be enjoying and how different your life would be if you were to overcome your fears.

3. Define your goal clearly. Focus on the results you want to produce; feel the fear – your knees wobbly, your stomach churning, your heart racing, the dryness of your mouth. Tell yourself that you can do it and then take bold, decisive action towards achieving your goals.

The World Eventually Sees What You See in the Mirror

*"What a man thinks of himself, that is which determines,
or rather indicates his fate."*

**Henry David Thoreau -
American Author, Poet, Naturalist and Philosopher**

There is a scene in *Cool Runnings* where Yul Brenner drags Junior Bevil into the restroom. Yul was disgusted by the docility with which Junior Bevil had allowed the East German, Josef Grull, reputed to be one of the best bobsled drivers in the world, to ridicule and taunt him. It was clear that Grull didn't believe that the Jamaicans belonged and was not shy about voicing his opinion. Yul could no longer suffer the insults, especially the attacks launched directly at his friend, so he dragged Junior into the rest room and planted him in front of the mirror.

"When you look in the mirror, what do you see?" He demanded. Confused, all Junior could mutter was *"Junior Bevil."*

Yul continued *"You know what I see? I see pride, I see power, I see a bad-ass mother who takes no crap from nobody."* Even more confused, Junior asked *"You really see that?"*

"Yes, Mon!" Yul responded emphatically. *"But it doesn't matter what I see. It's what you see that is important."*

After some encouragement, Junior Bevil finally saw himself as a bad-ass mother who didn't take crap from anyone. It is a very comical scene which underlines a simple and powerful truth: Others eventually see in you precisely how and what you see in yourself. Initially, they will not always see you the way you see yourself, simply because people tend to see us through their own colored prism, prejudices and preconceived ideas. That is just the way society is. We paint each other with these broad strokes which are often incorrect. Just think of some of the stereotypical views that you are aware of and you will see what I mean. What are some of the general assumptions that are out there about Asians, Blacks, Whites, people with AIDS? What immediately comes to your mind when you hear about immigrants or poor people? What images immediately pop into your head when you hear the word accountant, lawyer, or sales-man? I am quite aware that the general view is that everyone in Jamaica smokes weed and has dreadlocks, but I know for a fact that that is not true. A few years ago I was at a party in Salt Lake City when someone lit up a blunt and started passing it around the room. Everyone was surprised when I declined to partici-pate. I have never smoked a joint in my life and see no reason to start now. People will straight away assume they know what you are capable of simply because of how you look or where you are from. Eventually though, their opinion of you will match the opinion you have of yourself.

I am often asked if the movie's depiction of other teams' re-action to us was accurate. The answer is no. Besides, as a people we are proud. Very proud. We would strongly reject the kinds of taunts and abuses depicted in *Cool Runnings*. In any event, it has been my experience, both from competing in and watching sports across the board, that athletes do not treat each other that way. Even in extreme circumstance, where one team or athlete may intensely dislike the other, you would not see the kind of taunting that was displayed in *Cool Runnings*. Professional boxing and wrestling are the only times we would witness that sort of behavior, and, as we know, that is all showmanship. The only major race we competed in before the Olympics was a World Cup Race in Igls, Austria in November, 1987. During that race, we were forced to lift our sleds over those of other teams in order to make our way to the start line. A start list is always posted for every practice session and race. Your position on the list gives you the approximate time you will get on the track once the training session or race begins. It takes roughly two minutes once the track is cleared for the team to push off from the start, get to the bottom and lift the sled from the track. So, let's say that your starting position is fifteen. It means that you can expect to be on the starting blocks approximately thirty minutes after sliding commences.

A few minutes before the race gets underway, the team with the first starting position will be directed to put their sled on the ice. Just like in baseball, the next three sleds would be placed "on deck" a few feet behind the starting blocks lined up in the correct order. All the other teams in the race would take their cue from this and start moving their sled towards the on deck circle as the race progresses. Of course, this requires vigilance, as no one is going to come and call you. During that World Cup race in Igls, our team had no helpers; we were warming up and getting ready for the race and still had to figure out when it was time to move our sled. The other teams had more resources than we did. They had helpers whose primary responsibility was to get the sled up to the start line while their athletes only concerned themselves in preparing for the race. We were doing it all and found ourselves out of place and had to lift our sleds over everyone else's in order to get back in our proper order. I did not construe that to mean that the other teams were being unkind. We were inexperienced, but to suggest ill treatment from the other teams made a better story in Hollywood.

Back in 1987, most people found it difficult to imagine that Jamaica could have a bobsled team. Not only because of the stereotypical view I described earlier, but also because they had never heard the words "Jamaica" and "bobsled" used in the same sentence before. Their own limiting beliefs suggested to them that that was impossible. In Europe, people would see four black guys walking down the street dressed in similar jackets and ask if we were American basketball players. They would eye us suspiciously when we told them we were Jamaican bobsledders. Once, a guy enquired about who we were and I told him that we were uphill skiers from the Congo. He seemed intrigued so I went on to explain that we chose that sport because going uphill was even more difficult that going downhill. He believed it. Fact is indeed stranger than fiction. In their minds, a Jamaican is someone who is chilling on the beach sipping umbrella drinks and rocking to a steady stream of reggae music. They saw our team as a media stunt that didn't have the ability to bobsled and had no business being on the slopes. Some saw us as too easy going and laid back to deal with the rigors of a sport like bobsledding, while others saw us as party animals who were just there to have a good time.

This is the sort of thing that happens when people paint you with a broad stroke. They assume they know you when in reality they do not, and the biggest mistake you can make is to live down to their expectations. We had a completely different view of ourselves. The fact that you were raised in the *barrios* or the *hood* does not make you a gang banger or destined to become one. How can you not be inspired by Sonia Sotomayor, who was raised in a Bronx housing project by a widowed mother and yet rose to become the first Hispanic on the Supreme Court? Or Jose Hernandez? His remarkable journey has taken him from the fields of California, where he harvested crops and moved from town to town as a member of a migrant family from Mexico, to being an astronaut aboard the space shuttle *Discovery*.

We were not just Jamaicans. Like the others, we were athletes with the talent and the ability to become world class bobsledders. We worked hard and were voracious learners. Today, people have fully warmed up to the idea of a Jamaican bobsled team and are always excited to hear that we still have a team. Just as important, though, is the fact that our team has won the respect and admiration of many in the bobsled community. It is gratifying to hear the American driver Todd Hays, minutes after he had won the silver medal in the four-man race at the Salt Lake City Olympics, saying that the Jamaicans are awesome and he watches them to learn how to push. Only a few short years earlier the Americans were teaching us how to push a bobsled. During that time, however, as a team we continued to see ourselves with the ability to compete with the best in the sport. While we still have a long way to go, I think people are beginning to see what we have always seen in ourselves.

CHAPTER 17

What Is Self Image?

"A strong, positive self-image is the best possible preparation for success."

**Dr. Joyce Brothers -
American Psychologist and Advice Columnist**

I f you were to walk down any street in your hometown and poll everyone you met, you would discover that almost every person you spoke to wants more out of life. Whatever it is, they want more of it. They want to do it faster, better, and with less effort. But for the most part it doesn't happen. Why not? Success – rising to the top – requires us to be *different*, to stand out from the crowd, to risk failure, rejection and ridicule. Most people have a faulty self image, and it will not allow them to put themselves out there in any way. It kills their dreams long before they have a chance to take off. It buries their hopes and dashes their aspirations and so, although they want more, they never get it.

A good work ethic, courage, integrity, knowledge, skills, and how you conduct yourself all shine brightly in the marketplace. However, how you think about yourself and the person you see yourself to be when you are out of the limelight shines even brighter, has more relevance and determines the effectiveness in which you employ your knowledge and skills in the marketplace. Psychologists refer to this as your self image. Your self image is the person you see yourself to be with the abilities you believe you have. Often called your inner mirror, your self image is a product of past experiences, successes and failures, humiliations, triumphs and the way other people react to you, especially in early childhood. Your self image is the most dominant factor that affects everything you do. How you perform in any area of your life is only partly a function of your potential and largely a function of how you see yourself to be. In other words, you could have all the skill and training you will ever need. You could read all the self-help books you could find, spend your days attending peak performance seminars and have the world's greatest life coach advising your every move, but unless you see yourself winning in the game of life, you will not be half as successful as you could have been.

Everyone has an overall image of themselves as a person. You also have several miniature self images. A combination of your self image as a son or daughter, employee, entrepreneur, friend, parent, sibling, spouse, and so on makes up the overall person you see yourself to be. Even if you had all the will power in the world, you can never perform at a higher level than what you see yourself to be. Many vehicles are fitted with a governor to limit their speed. Many performance cars, for example, are limited to a speed of 155 mph. Urban public buses often have speed governors which are typically set between forty and sixty mph. In the same way that a governor limits the performance of a vehicle, no matter what it is capable of, your self image establishes the boundaries of your accomplishments. It decides what you can and cannot be, how you see yourself and ultimately how others view you. Broaden your self image and you in turn broaden what is possible for you.

I am sure that you could find scores of managers who will tell you of an employee who they thought had a lot of potential. This person has everything going for them. They are likeable, punctual and have integrity. They are encouraged and are given every opportunity to prove themselves, yet demonstrate time and time again that they are incapable of raising their game. Some parents have the same challenge with their kids. They are showered with love and attention and bought every toy and video game they could want and yet they perform way below their potential. Perhaps that person is you. How could someone be given the encouragement and opportunity to succeed and still fail? It happens because the reflection in their inner mirror does not show someone who is capable. Their preconceived negative beliefs and expectations create mental road blocks convincing them beforehand that their limitations, which of course are self-imposed, preclude them from succeeding.

People with poor self images are quite capable of superior performances, but they have found themselves locked in a vicious cycle. Their poor self image results in poor performances and those results confirm in their minds that that is all they are capable of. As a result of the failure-oriented self image they have developed, they find themselves locked in a downward spiral of sub-par performances. For example, a salesman might be given a fertile territory in an affluent neighborhood in which to build his business. If he believes that rich people are cheats and would not listen to him because he was born on the wrong side of the tracks, even though he took the time to set up the appointments, he will find a way to cancel them or, if he keeps them, find a way not to make the sale. The fact that his manager thinks the salesman has excellent selling skills and his potential client finds him to be a warm, personable individual is irrelevant. From the very moment he meets with his potential client, subconsciously he will begin to look for or *manufacture* the outward signs that will support his preconceived negative beliefs and expectations. These signs would eventually disturb his concentration, diminish his confidence and increase his nervousness – all to allow himself to fail. The salesman allows himself to become so distracted by the thought of failing, and the embarrassment of not closing the sale, that he actually brings it about. Likewise, the student who sees herself as bad at math or science, even when provided with all the tools to succeed, will validate her lack of ability in those subjects with the poor grades on her report card. The boy who thinks nobody likes him will behave in a way that will not endear him to others. When he does not receive an invitation to the hot party that everyone else will be attending, he becomes convinced that his suspicions were correct.

This same scenario is often played out in other areas as well. Though the girl's teachers think that she is exceptionally smart and has a lot of potential, or the boy's parents think that he is warm and friendly is inconsequential. None of them will succeed because of the poor opinions they have of themselves. The lesson here is that everyone you meet will have an opinion of you. In the final analysis, those opinions, whether they are good, bad or indifferent, have very little relevance to your ultimate success. The only opinion that matters is the one you have of yourself. Of the thousands of opinions you will ever have on hundreds of different subjects during your lifetime, the most important opinion you will ever have is the one you have of yourself. People with a negative self image live their lives without ever utilizing their full array of talents and abilities, and even the ones that are used are employed in such a way to ensure that they just get by. These people occupy a very tiny, restrictive world and in my mind aren't really living. They are merely existing. On the other hand, those with a positive self-image are more open to explore their full potential and take risks. They are the ones that grab life by the proverbial horns.

HOW YOUR SELF IMAGE IS DEVELOPED

When you are born your self-image is like a blank compact disc-neither good nor bad. The influences you have been exposed to and the experiences you have had, especially during childhood, get written on it. Children are particularly susceptible to the influences of their environment and the authority figures in their lives. Parents, teachers, family members and friends at some point might have called them "clumsy", "stupid", "slow", "fat", "smart", "a super star", "kind", "awesome", etc. Since children, as a rule, do not contradict authority figures, they simply internalize and accept these judgments as true. Especially the false, negative ones.

I suppose the need to feel like we belong and the pressure society puts on us to fit in cause us, even into adulthood, to feed our inner critic or our inner cheerleader. As a result you find yourself in a constant state of either criticizing and berating or praising and encouraging yourself. This inner dialogue either builds a positive self concept or a negative one. True or false, positive or negative, regardless of the influences and messages you have been bombarded with you are ultimately responsible for your own self image. In the end, you have the power to accept or reject what is said to you. You and you alone hold the key to your success or the lack of it. Do not get preoccupied with what others think of you. The world at large ultimately forms its opinion of you primarily from the opinion you have of yourself. What you see in yourself is what you get out of yourself. What you present yourself to be in the end is what is drawn out of you and what everyone else sees.

A number of years ago, I was in Los Angeles speaking at a school for teenage felons and delinquents. As I waited to address the group, I noticed a number of self portraits the students had done. As I wandered around the room looking at their work, I was impressed by its quality and the level of talent they had displayed. As I continued to be awed by the pieces, I began to wonder to myself what exactly it was that these kids saw as they looked in the mirror to paint themselves. Did they only see the things that genetics had given them? The color of their eyes, the size of their noses, the shape of their lips? Or were they seeing a little deeper? Did they see the image that people in their lives had painted of them? I secretly hoped that they were able to see even deeper. I hoped that they were able to look beyond genetics and the pictures that everyone else painted of them. I wished that they could somehow move away from their past – the negative judgments and inner critics – to see the winner that was inside of them just waiting to be awakened and take charge of their lives. They needed to know that they were powerless to do anything about what happened in the past, but that they had complete control over how they saw themselves and what they believed about themselves today and that that would be the game changer in their lives.

I felt compelled to explore those issues with those kids. Like me, they grew up in a poor environment. In fact, just the week before I visited with these kids, I was in Jamaica and had gone back to the old neighborhood. Most of the guys I grew up with were still there. Over the years, I had gone around the world while they had only gone around the block. It appeared that all their lives, whenever they looked in the mirror all they saw were misery and poverty and these two fellows have been their loyal companions all this time. Olympic Gardens is more popularly known as Waterhouse, but has been called Firehouse because it is volatile and often violent. It is place filled with broken down shacks set in a maze of dirt tracks and alleys. If you go there now you will see where they have made efforts to give the place a face lift, but to me it still looks dreary and run down. It is still a very economically depressed neighborhood, susceptible to flare ups of gang violence and senseless murders. It is the typical story;

some of the people I grew up with are in prison, some have been killed, but more than thirty years after leaving high school, most are still there. Whenever I go back to the old neighborhood, it is always great to see the people I know. But on the other hand, I wished they had moved on to bigger and better things. As I stop to say my hellos and to ask how they are doing, in the back of my mind I cringe at the thought that I could still be living there all these years under those conditions and wonder how they do it. But, of course, I know the answer. It is clear that they don't see a life for themselves beyond Waterhouse.

I am often asked about this. How was I able to rise above the circumstances under which I grew up and achieve the things I've done while many of my peers are still anguishing in the old neighborhood? We all went to the same schools, were subjected to the same influences and had similar opportunities; what made the difference? I think it begins with self image. I just could not see myself living under those conditions for the rest of my life. My self image allowed me to put myself out there and to deal with the discomfort of reaching beyond Waterhouse. While I was serving in the Jamaica Defence Force, my unit had a family day. Officers and men were encouraged to invite their family members and friends on the base for a day of fun and frolic. I was unmarried at the time, so I invited my siblings who were all younger. Naturally, they were invited to the officer's mess. After a while, I noticed that they were nowhere to be found. I went looking for them and eventually found them hanging out in the enlisted men's canteen. They didn't like being in the officer's mess with all those *rich people*. I marched them right back to the officer's mess. I was an officer and that's where they belonged. I understood their discomfort. It was the same one I felt when I returned from Sandhurst. I felt uneasy sitting at the same table and sharing a meal with men who, if things were different, would be in my old neighborhood holding me at gun point and strip searching me as they conducted one of the raids looking for wanted men and illegal weapons. I constantly had to remind myself that I belonged. I had earned it.

This still doesn't explain why I had a healthier self image than my peers. Why did they choose to live in a very restrictive way and take such small steps while I chose to take bigger risks? I still don't know the answer. What I do know, though, is that when you dare to expand the image you see in the mirror, it grows with every success you attain and challenges you to chase even bigger goals. Today, I am pursuing goals I never could have dreamt were possible growing up in Olympic Gardens. Writing this book and hopefully impacting the lives of millions of people around the world is one of them. That is one of the things I see when I look in the mirror.

*Opening ceremonies at the Minami Nagano Sports Park stadium in Nagano, Japan 1998. **(Front Row left to right:** Jason Morris, Dudley Stokes, Ernie Cosman, Michael Morgan. **Back Row left to right:** Ricky McIntosh, Dusty Miller, Devon Harris, Chris Stokes).*

CHAPTER 18

Developing a Positive Self Image

"Think highly of yourself,
for the world takes you at your own estimate."
Unknown

However we chose to define it, we all aspire to be successful. Success provides something everyone craves:
approval and acceptance. This strongly supports high
self esteem and a positive self image. The reverse is also true.
You need to maintain an adequate self image in order to lead
a satisfying and successful life. Maintaining a positive self image allows you to acknowledge your strengths and weaknesses
and still feel good about yourself. It enables you to feel free to
express yourself creatively rather than being ashamed of who
you are, and thirdly it keeps you grounded in reality so that you
can function effectively in society. On this last point, however,
I think that there are exceptions. I believe that really successful
people are slightly delusional. At least in the beginning, anyway.
There are five billion people living on the planet. Of that number, only about 13,000 get to compete in the Summer and Winter
Olympic Games in thirty-three different sports and nearly 400

events. As you know, only three medals are awarded in each event. I think you start off with a slightly delusional self image if you believe that, out of five billion people, you can win one or more of the only twelve hundred medals being awarded at the Olympic Games. Curiously, as you work towards that goal, and as you begin to achieve success in your chosen sport, your self image becomes stronger and stronger. In time, you find that you have not only beaten the odds and are marching in the opening ceremony of the Olympic Games, but you may become one of the select few who gets to stand on the medal podium.

If you choose to, there is nothing in the world that can prevent you from developing a healthy self-image. Needless to say, there is not much you can do about how you saw yourself in the past, but you have absolute control over how you see yourself from this day forward.

How do you picture yourself?

How do you feel about yourself?

What does it take to improve your self image?

As we discussed before, you form a mental picture of yourself through experience. Similarly, the way to change it is not through intellect or willpower but through experience. According to self-image psychology, if the actual experience we need is not available to us we can create that experience. That is to say, developing a positive self-image is an inside job. It begins with you accepting yourself for what you really are – one of a kind, as unique and different from anyone else as your fingerprint.

We know that there are myriad things that we are not good at. Stop focusing on them. Take some time to identify your strengths. Once you start taking an inventory of your finer qualities, you'd be surprised at how many you will find. This little exercise will begin the process of shifting your self image from negative to positive because you will discover that you already possess many of the qualities that you like and admire in others. It is important for you to remember that the main difference between you and the people you look up to is that they have already figured out how to achieve their goals and you haven't, as yet. You have been blessed with similar attributes and talents, and therefore success is as possible for you as it was for them. This enlarging of your self-image in turn improves your performance. Pursuing and achieving new goals require a healthy self-image and sometimes, as in the case of our bobsled team, you might even find yourself out of your league. The odds were stacked heavily against us and, as you know, we were constantly reminded of it. After we took an inventory of the qualities we possessed that would allow us to be good bobsledders, we concluded that we had desire, passion, a good work ethic and speed. We made up for our lack of experience and equipment with those qualities and proved to be very competitive. So start focusing on your good qualities and stop building a case against yourself. That's a job for others.

THOUGHTS ARE THINGS

You need to harbor the thoughts that would create and promote positive images of yourself. The late Earl Nightingale remarked that "You become what you think about most of the time." I use this line often during my presentations. A number of years ago, after I got off stage a guy came up to me to say that he disagreed with the statement. He went on to make the point that if you became what you think about most of the time, he'd be a woman by now! What can I say? Nothing in life is easy.

Your thoughts are really the inner dialogue you have with yourself. What subject do you discuss the most in the conversations you have with yourself? How do you think those conversations affect the way you see yourself? As author and stock analyst Ralph Charell said, "The inner speech, your thoughts, can cause you to be rich or poor, loved or unloved, happy or unhappy, attractive or unattractive, powerful or weak."

Unlike Junior Bevil in *Cool Runnings*, most of us would never allow anyone to belittle and berate us and get away with it, but it is shocking to know the kinds of horrible self deprecating things we say to ourselves every day. If the demeaning words that came out of your own mind about yourself were uttered by a stranger, you probably would hurt them. If those same words were aimed at your child, best friend, or some other person you cared about, like Yul Brenner, you would have ran to their defense. You would refuse to have anything to do with such a person or, in the very least, think that person was nuts. Yet people speak to themselves that way every single day. I cringe every time I hear someone say out loud "I am so stupid", "I am such a klutz"; "I just can't do anything right"; the list goes on. I understand the temptation for someone to yell out "I am so stupid" when they have messed up. I used to do it as well. Thankfully, I have learned that I can hold myself accountable, push myself and yet still be kind to myself. Let me encourage you to do the same. The most powerful words you will ever utter are the ones that come after "**I AM.**" Start paying close attention to what those words are. They determine whether your self image is negative or if it is one that is positive and supports your quest for greatness.

IGNORE THE EXPERTS

All of us have had to deal with the "experts" in our lives. They are those people who seem to believe they know what it is we can or cannot do and see it as their job to let us know. However well intentioned they might be, they are severely flawed because they cannot possibly know what is buried in your heart, your mind and your soul and hence what is being reflected in the mirror when you stand in front of it. We could all learn a valuable lesson from the bumble bee. For many years, it was "known" that the bumble bee was incapable of flying. Some of the best scientific minds in the world were able to prove this mathematically. The experts postulated that the wings of the bumble bee were too small and its body too big, therefore it was impossible for the bee to fly. Luckily for the bee, it had a vastly different view of itself and its abilities. It somehow *knew* that it was made to fly and despite all the scientific proof to the contrary, it managed to pull it off. The bumble bee proved that worrying about what others might think of you is an utter waste of time. If you allow yourself to believe and adopt the images that they have of you, you can never become what they think you are. You can only become and live up to the images that you have of yourself. And in the end they will see and accept that image as well.

What I am speaking about is not merely positive thinking. Merely thinking that you are capable of tremendous success is not enough. The image you hold of yourself determines the level of your performance and ultimately the level of your success. By the way, just as you cannot perform above the level that you see yourself, your self image will not allow you to perform below what you see yourself as capable of for too long either. The more powerful your self image, the more you are likely to scrape, crawl and persevere in order to live up to that image. Success dictates that you evaluate yourself not on what other people think of and see in you, but what you think of and see in yourself. Personally, I gratefully acknowledge when someone tells me that I am awesome, smart, intelligent, talented and so on. If they happen to tell me that I suck, I just assume that they don't know what they are talking about.

The quest for achievement often brings with it the need to pursue things you are not yet sure how to do. There is always a learning curve-knowledge that must be acquired, skills that need to be developed. I may admit to myself that I suck for the moment, but **I KNOW** that I am smart and talented enough to figure out what I need to learn and do to get the job done. That was certainly the case with our team as we worked to compete in Calgary. A healthy self image acknowledges only one true expert – the one you see in the mirror.

MAINTAINING A WINNING ATTITUDE

It is well within your ability to grow into the person you desire to be. That is why it is so important for you to set goals. However, you cannot afford to have the future completely occupy your mind no more than you can allow your thoughts to be dominated by past events and experiences. Undoubtedly, both are useful. Future goals provide us with energy and motivation and a drive to get past the obstacles in order to achieve them. Past success represents a time when we overcame a challenge and won.

These victories, large and small, reinforce a positive self image and provide positive proof that we have the ability to succeed. Winners, however, are more responsive to the present. They use the strength of their past successful experiences and the pull of future goals to solve their current problems and chart a path to higher levels of achievement. Embracing a strong self image and a positive concept of yourself is essential to maintaining a winning attitude. As Maxwell Maltz, author of *Psycho-Cybernetics*, wrote: "Our self image, strongly held, essentially determines what we become"

AFFIRM YOURSELF

So what hope is there for you if you find yourself haplessly living down to the standards set for you by others? How do you rebound from a negative self image? We know that we were born with unlimited potential and the ability to succeed through hard work, courage, determination and faith. We know that we were not given a negative self image at birth but that, over time, our self image was developed through a combination of conditioning and affirmation. Over the years we've listened to, accepted and believed what others have said about us. We have even taken some of the limitations they have placed on themselves and adopted them as our own. In time, we have become conditioned to see ourselves a certain way and we affirm this negative image of ourselves.

Growing up in a violent, economically depressed area was challenging. Many people lost hope so badly that they began to call themselves *sufferers*. Several of the boys I grew up with resorted to this practice, but it was not one I could embrace. I looked around me and saw what happened to sufferers. They were locked in a holding pattern of poverty and misery and I couldn't imagine being doomed to a life like that. As a result I disassociated myself from those guys.

There is a mysterious and powerful force known as affirmation. Affirmations are words that others say to you or that you say to yourself that you have come to believe. Once you truly believe them you begin to form your self image and, like clockwork, you always act in a manner consistent with your self image. As a barefooted boy running track in high school, I consistently told myself: "I am the best! I am the best!" I believed I was the best at my school and consequently I never lost to anyone from my school. Despite my fear of speed I talked myself into becoming a world class bobsled driver. That was simply how I saw myself. As if bobsledding wasn't difficult enough, I have chosen to live my life as a motivational speaker. Statistics have shown that more people would prefer to die rather than speak in front a room full of people. Yet I find myself traveling around the world, sometimes speaking to rooms filled with thousands of people. I am often asked if I am ever nervous when I speak, and the answer is yes. I usually feel nervous as I am getting ready to take the stage and remain so for the first few minutes. The bottom line is that I see myself as a very competent speaker. As I mentioned before, I always imagine myself on stage; calm, relaxed, confident, totally at ease, charming, engaging, passionate. I am no longer surprised when audience members tell me how relaxed and at ease I seem on stage. I already saw it in the mirror.

By feeding your mind positive, empowering thoughts you eventually create a powerful empowering self image. This translates into an unshakable belief in your abilities and causes you to exude an aura of confidence. It is mirrored in everything you do, and after a while, despite their predispositions others will see it as well. They just can't help themselves.

KEY POINTS TO REMEMBER - LESSON 6

- Initially, people tend to see you only through their own colored prism, prejudices and preconceived ideas. Eventually, however, what they see in you reflects precisely how you see and think of yourself.

- Your self-image, or inner mirror, reveals the kind of person you see yourself to be with the abilities you believe you have. It is a product of past experiences, successes and failures, humiliations, triumphs and the way other people react to you.

- Your self-image does to you what governors do to vehicles: It establishes the boundaries of your accomplishments. Therefore, how you perform is only partly a function of your potential and largely a function of how you see yourself to be. Broaden your self image and you in turn broaden what is possible for you. (continued on page 184)

KEY POINTS TO REMEMBER - LESSON 6

- Your preconceived negative beliefs and expectations create mental road blocks convincing you beforehand that your limitations preclude you from succeeding.

- Everyone you meet will have an opinion of you. In the final analysis, those opinions, whether they be good, bad or indifferent, are not important. The only opinion that matters is the one you have of yourself. That is the most important opinion you will ever have.

- People with a negative self-image live their lives without ever utilizing their full array of talents and abilities, and even the ones that are used are used only enough for them to simply get by. The more powerful your self image, the more open you are to explore your full potential, take risks and persevere until you succeed.

ASSIGNMENTS

1. Compile a detailed list of the good habits you possess and the things you like about yourself.

2. Quit thinking negatively about yourself and comparing yourself to others. Instead, constantly think about and remind yourself of all your good qualities and the things you like most about yourself.

3. Spend time every day visualizing yourself as the person you would like to be with the abilities and attributes you would like to have.

4. Try new things. Gradually step out of your comfort zone.

Twists and Turns Are Natural Parts of the Course

"We are built to conquer environment, solve problems, achieve goals, and we find no real satisfaction or happiness in life without obstacles to conquer and goals to achieve."
Maxwell Maltz - Cosmetic Surgeon and Author

One, two, three, four. They are all in. Four men each, weighing more than 200 pounds, running as fast as their legs will take them, jumping into a tiny sled in flawless synchronicity. All the heads are lowered except for the driver's. He is looking steadfastly ahead, anticipating what is before him. Oblivious to the frenzy of the crowds, the vibrations of the sled or the rattling of the runners on the ice as he gently squeezes the ropes and guides the sled down the track. The sled meanders slowly through corner one, and two, crawls into three and, almost without warning, tears through four. That's where the real excitement begins as the sled picks up speed in excess of seventy-five mph. Before the sledders know it, they have already completed turn five as they scream through a long looping right hand turn in corner six. As they hit the curves the g-forces start to increase. One g-force is approximately one time your body weight. Can you imagine a force of four or five times your body weight pushing your head down between your knees? The athletes are still gasping for breath after the all-out sprint and hard pushing at the start. The g-forces compress their diaphragms, making it even more difficult to breathe. As the sled comes off the corner it slams hard into the wall – Bam! Believe me…it takes your breath away. In less than sixty seconds you've covered the mile long course. Sheer exhilaration.

In my mind, a bobsled track is one long obstacle course of twists and turns, where successful completion requires courage, diligence and focus on each turn. Challenging and intimidating, these corners are almost daring you to avoid them; but if you take the bait, you do so at your own peril. It is impossible to get down the track by ignoring even the smallest, shortest corner. Physicists will tell you that centripetal force is the external force required to make a body follow a curved path. If a driver tries to avoid the corner by forcing the sled to stay in the bottom of the track, the centripetal forces will pull on it so hard that the sled flips over. I learned that lesson very early on in my bobsled career. It was only a few weeks after we first went on ice. We were still in Calgary learning to get from the top of the track to the bottom safely. Finish times were not a concern at that point in our training. On one of our runs, on the lower half of the track, Sammy entered one of the corners far too late. Missing the entry point of a corner, or what in bobsledding we call the "take on," always makes for an interesting ride. As a general rule, the driver is always trying to stay in the middle of the straightways. If he is approaching a left-hand turn (the turn is physically on the right of the track, but the driver has to steer to the left to navigate it) he wants the sled to be just to the right of center. In the vernacular we say the sled should be *tracking middle-right*. If he is approaching a right-hand turn he wants to be tracking middle-left. In this instance, we were too far to the right. In bobsled jargon, we were sliding down the right wall. When we got to the entrance, the corner pushed us away. In essence, because we were so close to the right wall, as the straight wall transitions into the corner the front bumper of the sled hits the wall, causing us to completely miss the take on. Instead of allowing the pressure to pull the sled back up on the corner, Sammy figured that he would force his way around on the belly, which is how we refer to the bottom of the track. He had the front runners of the sled locked in a left-hand turn while the centripetal force was pulling the sled to the right. The huge battle between man and nature saw the sled climb the corner steeply and we flipped over.

This was my first crash, and although it happened in a split second, it felt as if it lasted minutes. You first get this strange sensation. It is difficult to explain, but the sled feels like it is moving in slow motion. It is almost like you are having an out-of-body experience. You are watching and feeling your body in silence move slowly through time and space, flip over and hit the ice, but the minute your head hits the ice everything speeds up again. Your senses are heightened and your survival instincts kick in. You can feel the sled whipping violently around the corners; you can see the white ice flashing by, smell the fiber glass burning as the horrible sound of the sled scraping over the ice pierces your ears.

CHAPTER 19

It's an Obstacle Course to the Finish Line

"By prevailing over all obstacles and distractions, one may unfailingly arrive at his chosen goal or destination."
Christopher Columbus -
Italian Navigator, Colonizer and Explorer

It is never easy to navigate even the most uncomplicated of these turns. Because bobsledding is a sport where one hundredth of a second could mean the difference between winning a medal and being shut out of the medal standings, it is of paramount importance that even the smallest, shortest corner is driven with precision and care. Driving requires complete focus on the corner you are navigating. Thinking of the mistake you made in the corner you just left behind, or casting your thoughts on the one that's just up ahead, is asking for trouble. While traveling at 100 mph in a car, you can adjust the rear view mirror or the dials on the radio, engage in a lively conversation on the phone or with the passenger beside you without any real danger of meeting in an accident. In bobsledding, because you are so close to the ground and you almost feel like you are surrounded by the track, going at eighty mph feels incredibly fast. Allowing your thoughts to be on anything except the corner you are driving will more than likely result in a crash.

No two tracks are the same, although there are many similarities between tracks. For example, although it falls away more steeply, turn six in Park City is similar to turn seven in Calgary; while corner four in Igls, Austria and corner two in Nagano, Japan are similar. The tracks range from 1220 meters in length to over 1600 meters. By rule the steepest part of any track cannot be more than sixteen percent, and, as you can imagine, because they are built on different terrain, gradient differs significantly. They also vary in the number of turns – fourteen in Nagano, Japan to twenty in Lake Placid, New York. Because of these differences, there are no world records in bobsledding. Each course boasts a start record and a track record.

Imagine that a bobsled track was just a straight icy chute that ran for a mile or so down the side of a mountain. Where would the fun or challenge be in that? How would you test a driver's courage and ability? Apart from being able to push faster at the start, how would a team be able to catch up or increase their advantage over their nearest competitor? It is the corners, with their varying degrees of difficulty, combined with focus and the skills required to navigate them that makes it such an exigent and exhilarating sport. The fun and the attraction to the sport are in the challenges that these many twists and turns present. Without them, bobsledding would simply be drag-racing on ice.

The road of life is also a long, continuous journey of twists and turns – challenges that we must become adept at handling in order to hit our goals. There is no doubt that life would be a whole lot easier without these obstacles, but, as it turns out, the path to our goals, growth and success is strewn with them. Like those on a bobsled track, life's twists and turns are nerve-wracking. However, it is safe to say that if you are not facing challenges, you are not living. As corny as it sounds, the only people I know who don't have to deal with any challenges are those lying in a cemetery. It is a natural for a business to experience cash flow problems, institute a hiring freeze or lay people off. It is natural for some workers to lose benefits, have their jobs outsourced or have their hours cut. It is natural to have conflicts in a relationship and for some of them to even end. Financial, emotional, health and physical challenges to varying degrees are all unavoidable parts of our life's experiences.

The universe has dictated that, in order to grow and succeed, we must make effort. Nothing that is accomplished too easily is truly appreciated. All of us tend to treasure and hold more dearly that which we accomplish through sweat, tears, creativity and innovation. Life's twist and turns have to be dealt with. They cannot be ignored. Those who learn to navigate them eventually hit their goals and move on to enjoy great success. Great accomplishments can only be achieved by scaling great obstacles. People who try to avoid them end up with even bigger problems. Shortcuts in business practices often lead to failure of the business. Avoiding conflicts in a relationship leads to a break up. Ignoring a medical issue leads to complications and ignoring the warning signs could lead to severe hardships. The list goes on.

CHAPTER 20

Learn to Navigate the Turns

"Obstacles don't have to stop you. If you run into a wall, don't turn around and give up. Figure out how to climb it, go through it, or work around it."
Michael Jordan - Basketball player

S ince there is simply no way to get from the top of a bob-sled track to the bottom without navigating the turns, the driver has to figure out how to steer the sled on and off them. As a novice driver, I used to look at the turns, especially at the narrow points where they meet the straight portions of the track and wonder how on earth I was ever going to make it through, especially at those high speeds. At first I reassured myself that I could do it simply because others have done it before. As it turned out, after I tackled my doubts and fears and started going down the track, I began to develop confidence in my own abilities. Since challenges are a part of everyday life, we might as well learn to deal with them effectively as well. The challenges you face in your life might be entirely new to you, but you can be sure that from time immemorial someone else has had to overcome a similar obstacle, and whatever others have done, you can do as well. That's your first reference point. The second point you have to become aware of is that you simply have to go out and do it. Success is experiential. You can't hire somebody to do your push ups for you and expect to develop bulging biceps. You can learn technique and form from someone else, but in the end you will have to do them yourself. Likewise, if you want to learn how to navigate the challenges in your life you have to take them on yourself. It is also pointless looking at someone else and concluding that it was easier for them to succeed because their challenges are not as daunting as yours. The truly great person is the one who has found a way to overcome their particular set of challenges.

In bobsledding, every effort is made to make the race as fair as possible; but the truth is that in the end the playing field is never and can never be completely level. In track and field everyone runs at the same time under the exact conditions. In most other sports, this remains true. All the competitors are in the game under precisely the same conditions. In bobsledding, you are at the mercy of the draw. Everyone covets it, but obviously only one team can get the number one starting position. While this doesn't guarantee you the victory, it is a decided advantage because every sled that comes after slides on slightly slower ice. It would be a total waste of time for the driver with start number ten to lament over his start number. He, like everyone else in the race, must find a way to win while overcoming his own unique set of challenges. Succeeding in life is no different.

Some of the strategies a bobsled driver employs to learn how to successfully negotiate the track can prove to be very useful to everyone as we seek to navigate life's twists and turns.

NAVIGATING TIP #1:
STUDY THE TRACK
As I mentioned before, a driver, regardless of his experience, does a track walk before practice sessions and competitions.

Each track presents its own unique set of challenges. There is always a "problem corner"– one that is more technically challenging than the others. The speed of the track, the number of turns, their length and combinations are all things that he has to be aware of.

By studying the track and each corner in particular the driver ends up with a good idea of what he needs to do to successfully steer through it. Because the tracks are similar in some ways, he is able to take what he knows about one track and apply it to another. Just like the twist and turns on a bobsled track, life's challenges are all unique; but the similarities prepare you to deal with each successive one. You may not be able to study your impending challenges the way a bobsled driver studies the corners on a track, but if you are planning your goals properly you should have a fairly good idea of the difficulties that lie ahead and prepare for them.

NAVIGATING TIP #2:
WATCH OTHER DRIVERS

Your ability to observe and learn from others is invaluable. Bobsled drivers spend a lot of time watching other drivers going down the track in order to see what they themselves need to do. You can also learn from others. Both from the mistakes they make and also from how they successfully scaled their challenges.

NAVIGATING TIP #3:
COACHES

A coach is of invaluable help to a driver. He stands by a particular corner and watches the sled as it goes by. He is then able to show the driver the lines he took through that corner and talk him through the appropriate adjustments. Hiring a personal coach or seeking a mentor will prove to be just as valuable to you.

NAVIGATING TIP #4:
DO IT

There is simply no substitute for effort and experience. You cannot learn to swim by reading a book or watching someone else do it. Likewise, you cannot learn to overcome life's challenges by simply watching someone else deal with their crisis. The only way to truly learn is by being courageous enough to face your challenges head-on. You have to do it.

After a bobsled driver has walked the track, watched other drivers, reviewed video tapes and listened to the advice of his coach, he has to get in the sled and figure out the nuances for himself. At first, he drives for survival – trying not to crash; and when he does, he goes back to the top and starts again. It is all part of the learning experience. You have to be bad before you're good. And you have to be good before you're great. Once he has steered the sled down the track a few times, he begins the never ending process of fine tuning his skills.

You and no one else is the captain of our ship. Once you have received advice, mentoring, financial support, and so forth-once you've been given your push start, your teammates, like the three guys in the back of the sled, can only provide you with moral support. It is up to you to guide your sled through the inevitable twist and turns ahead.

NAVIGATING TIP #5:
PATIENCE

For a sport that is synonymous with speed, it is difficult to reconcile the thought that bobsled drivers have to learn to be patient. It is always amusing to see the knitted brows on people's faces when I am explaining what happens in one of the turns. Oftentimes when you see a sled fly through a turn, the driver has steered three times; on longer corners, he has to exercise patience and resist the urge to steer the sled off the corner. Steering the sled off the corner too early will almost certainly end up in a crash.

Whenever you are in a crisis, I know there is nothing you'd like better than to have it over with. Oftentimes however, rushing to get to the light at the end of the tunnel can make things worse. Whether you are experiencing a slump in your business, a downturn in the economy, a long bout of illness or conflict in a relationship, it does take time to turn things around. Your best course of action is to make sure you are doing the things that will eventually resolve the issues and exercise a great deal of patience. Impatience will likely only make things even worse.

NAVIGATING TIP #6:
POSITIVE ATTITUDE

If you take a close look at the body language and the routine of the athletes standing on the starting blocks waiting for the track to be cleared, you will notice pronounced differences. The current number one driver in the world, Andre Langen of Germany, stands with his goggles in his hand, arms folded. His demeanor is so cool and calm it almost looks nonchalant. Nico Baracchi, who raced for Switzerland in the early nineties, rocks from side to side with a slight grin on his face, while his countryman Gustav Weder had a cold steely stare. The Americans shout at the top of their lungs, "C'mon, baby," while the British team is more subdued as they urge, "C'mon chaps." Whether they seem aggressive or reserved, one thing is for sure: They all possess an attitude of confident expectation. They embrace the challenge of the track – driving each corner with perfection and shaving every hundredth of a second that they can from their time. They also embrace the challenge of the race – opening up or at least maintaining the distance between them and their nearest competitor, or on the flip side closing the gap or passing the team ahead of them.

To be among the best at any endeavor, you have to maintain an attitude of confident expectation. You have to know deep inside that you are good at what you do and expect the best regardless of the challenges. While you accept that the journey of life will always have its twist and turns, it is important to note that oftentimes your biggest challenges are not necessarily out in the world. Most of the time, they are inside of you. It all comes down to how you think about and perceive the challenges you face. You cannot control the events that take place in your life. You cannot control the fact that Wall Street might be crumbling and several companies are going bankrupt. You cannot control how the government handles these challenges and the effects they will have on yourself. However, you can absolutely control how you respond to these events. It is all about your attitude. Renowned writer Chuck Swindoll reminds us that attitude, "Is more important than the past, than education, than money, than circumstances, than failures, than successes, than what other people think or say or do."

One of the best ways to develop an empowering attitude is to face your fears. As we discussed earlier, everyone has fears. From billionaires to barbers, from executive officers to executive assistants – none of us has been able to get through this economic crisis without feeling some sort of anxiety and fear. I was recently browsing through the FIBT website. On there they have a list of the fourteen bobsled tracks that are sanctioned around the world. I watched clips of the sled going down the track on each run from the driver's perspective. As I did so, I felt all the intense emotions as I did when I was the one sitting in the front of the sled, driving down the track. One of the strongest emotions I remember is fear. Most of us allow ourselves to get caught up in the fear, and in that state of mind you are already defeated. Fear is an emotion that can serve you. It is a call to action. It is telling you that, although you are experiencing a crisis, although there are challenges up ahead, you can still get through them. As I am going down the track, I empower myself with an attitude of confident expectation. I do not focus on the fear, but on exactly what I need to do to steer the sled on and off each corner. We are not supposed to get transfixed by the fear in our lives. It is telling us that we need to do something about the current challenges. Make what is not working right.

Secondly, take complete control of your thinking and concentrate on the solution rather than the problem. It is impossible for your mind to hold two diametrically opposite thoughts at the same time. Focus on the crisis – the loss or lack in your life and the fear generated by them will dis-empower you. Instead, concentrate your thoughts on your goals – how you would like things to be and what you need to do to make it so. You will find that a far more powerful place from which to operate and enable you to have a more positive disposition. Look for the good in every situation. Be positive and cheerful, no matter what happens.

A negative attitude cripples you by creating a tunnel vision of the problems you are facing. People who are solely focused on the hardships of these tough economic times will more than likely find their situation going from bad to worse. First their hours are cut back, then they are laid off, they get behind on bills and so on. Some will see these events as natural occurrences resulting from a downturn in the economy. While that may be true, it is largely true for those with a negative attitude. A poor attitude is almost a resignation or, at the very least, an acceptance that things will only get progressively worse. Someone with a positive attitude will see these same challenges as a great chance to start anew. A positive attitude allows you to see every challenge as an opportunity to ask yourself pertinent, soul-searching questions about what you want your life to be like. It is an opportunity to reassess your priorities and ultimately to grow.

Today, the bad economy fills the news with stories of bankruptcy and home foreclosures. It is also not unusual to hear stories of people who, because they are working less hours, learn a new skill or implement an innovative business idea. Although they were experiencing crises in their lives, by having a positive attitude, they were able to turn their situation around. As the American philosopher and psychologist William James once wrote, "Human beings, by changing the inner attitudes of their minds, can change the outer aspects of their lives." I believe that one way to do that is to resist the temptation of asking "Why?" People meet up on difficult times, and they expend their energy lamenting over what has befallen them. Here is a far more empowering alternative: Start asking yourself, "How?" Goal achieving and navigating the twists and turns in your life are nothing more than problem solving. If you want to get better at scaling the obstacles in your life, get better at problem solving. You don't solve problems by asking, "Why?" You do so by figuring out, "How?"

Members of the 1994 Lillehammer Olympic Team.
Left to Right-Front row: *Dudley Stokes, Ricky McIntosh, Wayne Thomas, Jerome Lewis* **Left to Right-Rear:** *Winston Watt, Chris Stokes*

CHAPTER 21

Feel the Rhythm

*"If we had no winter, the spring would not be so pleasant;
if we did not sometimes taste of adversity,
prosperity would not be so welcome."*
Anne Bradstreet - American Poet

As we know, there are several similarities between bobsled tracks and, of course, there are fundamental differences as well. The geographic locations, the length of the tracks, and the number of turns are just some of them. The corners on each track are laid out differently as well. The Lake Placid track has longer straightways, while the track in Koeniggssee, Germany is one swift turn after another. Some tracks have upper and lower labyrinths which are three short, quick consecutive turns, while others like La Plagne have back-to-back long, sweeping turns that pull so much g-forces even the driver is consciously aware of it. In essence, each track has it own rhythm and the driver must adjust to the rhythm of the track to negotiate it successfully.

Theoretically, a sled can make it all the way down the track without a driver steering it. In 1988, during official training for the two-man event, one of the Portuguese teams crashed on the upper half of the track. Miraculously, the sled came right side up a few corners later and we all watched in amusement as the sled made its way down the track and across the finish line without any input from the driver. When the sled crashed, he slid under the cowling and never bothered to raise his head and take hold of the steering ropes after the sled righted itself.

I am not sure that a sled could successfully make it down the track consistently on its own; if it could the times would be very slow. The best drivers in the world are those who have figured how to allow the sled to run its natural course on the track but also to tweak it just enough to find the fastest lines without crashing. Drivers are always dancing along the precarious boundary between fast lines and crash lines. Each corner prepares you for the ensuing one. A mistake in one corner is likely to follow you into the next. You can correct your mistake not by forcing the sled to go where you would like it to go but by relaxing, focusing your eyes on the part of the corner that you want to be and gently guiding the sled there. The best drivers have figured out how to flow with the rhythm of the track and keep their minds focused on the finish line.

There is always a natural tendency to fight to control every aspect of our lives. We also display a penchant to mire in self-pity when we are faced with difficulties ranging from job loss, bankruptcy to illness and everything in between. The bobsled driver goes with the flow of the track, tweaking the sled to find the fastest and safest lines. One of the ways you go with the flow of the universe when facing many of these challenges is to make the difficult decisions. If you are falling behind in your mortgage payments, maybe the difficult decision that you need to make is to sell your current home and downsize so that you don't go into bankruptcy and lose everything. If you have been laid off from your job and money is tight, perhaps the difficult decision you make is to take the kids out of private school and enroll them in public school or take a job that is far below your level of education and experience. Of course, these are less than ideal situations; but, as you know from bobsledding, forcing your way out of a problem is likely to make it worse. You have to be willing to take the less than ideal route, keep your mind on your goals and ease your way back on track. If one of your goals is the long-term financial stability of your family, then these are steps that you may have to take.

When my teammates and I were in Evanston, Wyoming delivering pizza, we often joked that this is not the kind of job that you put on your resume. We could have cried "foul" or whined "life is not fair," but that would not have put us any closer to achieving our goal of competing in the Olympics. Truth be told, privately and collectively we questioned whether or not we were doing the right thing – whether two retired Army captains and a university student were living up to their full potential by delivering pizza. Were we becoming worthless time wasters? It is difficult not to feel this way. If you had to trade in your warm, comfortable home in a suburban neighborhood for a cramped apartment in the city, or accept a position at the bottom of the totem pole after the corner office at your old company, it is difficult not to feel like a failure. But we have to accept that the rhythm of life changes with the seasons. As Jim Rhon states in his book *The Seasons of Life*: "Each day is given to us as a new season of spring. The thoughts dreams of today will provide tomorrow's harvest."

Summer presents its own sets of challenges and rewards. It is a time to protect what you have planted in the spring from the poisonous weeds and bugs that appear in the form of toxic opinions and poor advice and negativity around you. Accept that these things exist to test your will to succeed and your worthiness for life's rich rewards. You protect yourself through your determination and increased activity. If you planted well in the spring and worked hard in the summer to fight the bugs and weeds, you will reap the reward of a rich harvest in autumn. If you treated spring as leisure time; if you neglected to take massive action in the summer – directing your thoughts and actions towards changing your circumstances – then you will end up with a barren field in autumn. Then comes winter. It always come. Not only the winter of snow, ice and cold winds, but also the human winters of despair and disappointment, confusion and crisis, lack and loss.

Every one of us faces these challenges in our lives. But the one great thing about the cycle of life is that winter is always followed by spring. What follows the darkest night is the bright day. There is always calm after the storm. We always have a chance to start anew, a chance to prepare ourselves for what happens after the crisis and turmoil in our lives.

Our team kept focused on our goals and worked hard. Even though arguably we were going through a tough winter, we treated each day as spring time and that helped us to continuously look for the opportunities instead of sweating the difficulties. Goal-oriented people accept life's twist and turns and, through a positive attitude, are able to roll with the punches. Instead of adopting a "why does this have to happen to me?" approach they shift to a learning strategy. They see the inevitable obstacles as a chance to change their strategy and continue to work persistently to eventually achieve their desired outcome. They do not throw their hands up in despair nor hang their head in defeat. Smile favorably on the adversities in your life. They force you to grow. Know that your character is formed and strengthened not by the absence of difficulty in your lives but by your response to it.

KEY POINTS TO REMEMBER - LESSON 7

- The road of life is a long continuous journey of challenges, setbacks and obstacles that you must become adept at handling in order to hit your goals.

- Since challenges are a natural part of everyday life, achieving happiness and success at any level requires constant effort in order for you to learn to deal with them effectively.

- Nothing that is accomplished too easily is truly appreciated. Human beings tend to treasure and hold more dearly that which they accomplish through sweat and tears.

- Life's twist and turns cannot be avoided, swept aside or ignored. Those who learn to navigate them eventually hit their goals and move on to enjoy great success.

- There can be no real achievement without the test. Those who have had everything given to them, or have had it too easy, are emotionally unfit. They lack the deep sense of internal pride, strength and resilience that comes from experiencing challenges.

- Regardless of the arena you chose to compete in, you must to have attitude of calm, confident, positive self-expectation. You have to know deep inside that you are good at what you do and expect the best regardless of the challenges you are facing.

- A negative attitude cripples you by creating a tunnel vision of the problems you are facing. People who are solely focused on their hardships will more than likely find their situation going from bad to worse. Take complete control of your thinking and concentrate on the solutions you are seeking rather than the problems you are facing. No matter what happens, look for the good in every situation.

(continued on page 204)

204 Keep On Pushing: Hot Lessons From Cool Runnings

KEY POINTS TO REMEMBER - LESSON 7

- High achievers see the inevitable obstacles as an opportunity to change their strategy and continue to work persistently to eventually achieve their desired outcome.

ASSIGNMENTS

1. Accept and expect that the path to your goals will be strewn with disappointment.

2. Remain focused on your goals and feel the boost of energy they give you to overcome your obstacles.

Teamwork Makes the Dream Work

"There is no such thing as a self-made man.
You will reach your goals only with the help of others."
George Shinn - American Entrepreneur

I t is still surprising to me that so many people think the term "teamwork" only applies to athletes who play team sports. Such a narrow-minded view denies the fact that we've always had teammates, and when we work together to achieve a common goal, however insignificant it might be, that's teamwork. In school we used to sing a folk song with the following words, *"No man is an island. No man stands alone."* I doubt that at the time I really understood how true and powerful those words were. Over the years, I have come to realize that nothing of significance was ever achieved by one person acting alone. Teams come in all shapes and sizes and serve different purposes. Where would we be without our first teammates – our parents who loved and nurtured us during those early years? Where would we be without the guidance and support of teachers? What would we do without friends who meet our social and emotional needs, or coworkers who help us to grow professionally or our best friends whom we told our most intimate secrets? The examples of teammates we are surrounded by and how they have teamed up with us to help us grow in all areas of our lives are endless. Their role has been invaluable. We needed their insight, encouragement, strength, support and, even when it hurts, their honesty.

We often hear of the self-made person. The person who pulls his or herself up by the bootstraps. There is no doubt that your personal success begins and ends with you. You are the one who has to be motivated to achieve. You are the one who has to be willing to do the heavy lifting and to grind it out when times get tough. There can be no doubt about that. What needs to be just as clear, however, is the fact that you cannot do it all by yourself. The grandson of slaves who rose to become the nation's first African-American to sit on the Supreme Court, Thurgood Marshall demonstrated that he understood the important role others played in his success when he said, "None of us got where we are solely by pulling ourselves up by our bootstraps."

Ask any described, self-made person and they will tell you of the support and encouragement they received from parents, teachers, mentors and friends. There are more than enough examples of the Michael Jordans, the Bill Gates, the Margaret Thatchers, or the Mother Theresas of the world. You will find them in every field of human endeavor. Stalwarts who, through drive, personal ambition and a unique sense of purpose, have stood head and shoulders above the rest. And yet, no matter how exceptional they were or were deemed to have been, teamwork played a pivotal role in their development and achievements. They needed teammates in whom they believed and who believed in them. The richness and quality of our lives is in no small part due to the quality of the teammates we have chosen and the quality of the relationships we have developed with them. As speaker and author Brian Tracy once said, "Teamwork is so important that it is virtually impossible for you to reach the heights of your capabilities or make the money that you want without becoming very good at it."

Meeting members of the Chinese team during the Opening ceremony at the 1998 Nagano Games.

CHAPTER 22

Getting On the Sled

*"Lots of people want to ride with you in the limo,
but what you want is someone who will take the bus with you
when the limo breaks down."*

**Oprah Winfrey -
Media Personality, Actress and Television Producer**

The effort you put into selecting the people you want on your team is no less important than the time you invest in getting clear about the goals you want to pursue. Finding the right teammates is not an easy process and should never be taken lightly. Sports teams have trials where potential team members go through a rigorous selection process in order to be identified as new teammates. These people are selected for their athletic prowess in addition to their contribution and sphere of influence in the locker room as well as in the public domain. Their personality, ability to buy into the team's system, and their work ethic are just as important as their ability to support and encourage other team members. They also need to perform during clutch game situations to help the team win. Because of their importance to the team's overall success, teams tend to be cautious about who they eventually invite onto the team. Although it is not as easy and straightforward in the game of life, we need to be just as careful when we select our teammates. Granted, we do inherit some team members by default. Our parents and other family members simply come with the package, and while I do not mean to sound callous, when it comes to your personal success, they have to be put through the same rigorous selection process as anyone else. No matter how much you like them, not everyone can be first string on your team. There are some people in your life that you will have to love from a distance. They simply do not share your burning ambition and drive, and having them in your locker room will prove to be more like a ball and chain around your neck and not the wind at your back.

Professional athletes, because of their wealth and fame, are often in the news. And the majority of times when they find themselves in trouble, it can usually be traced back to the friends from the old neighborhood that they still hang out with. Despite the tremendous growth of their checkbooks, out of loyalty to the people they grew up with these athletes have stunted their own personal development and sometimes even find themselves on the wrong side of the law.

A few years ago, I was listening to a disc jockey in New York, and he shared a few pearls of wisdom on the subject. He said, "Some of the people who started with you cannot go with you."

Once again, some of you reading this might say this is cold-hearted. How can you ditch the people who you grew up with? But this is not about using people and casting them aside. Remember that you have a responsibility – you owe it to yourself to *Keep On Pushing* towards **YOUR** full potential. Some of us take that responsibility seriously, and others don't. We all grow in different ways because we all have different talents and interests. Nonetheless, we all have the innate ability for tremendous growth. If your family members and friends choose to be non-starters or joggers, that's their choice. You do what you can to help them, but you have to move on to find other pushers who can be on your team.

I grew up with two sets of peers – those in my neighborhood and those that I attended high school with. Unlike in the United States, high school in Jamaica is not a rite of passage. This was especially true during the period before the early 1970s. Prior to this period, a high school education was very costly and therefore not easily accessible to the poor. There were opportunities for those among the poorer class who excelled to receive a free high school education, but this accounted for only about five percent of the population. In the 1970s, the government began to build more schools. The elementary school I attended, for example, was only a year old when I enrolled. More high schools were built, and free places awarded to them. Theoretically, your education from elementary school all the way through to university could have been free. However, the path to one of these free places in high school led through the Common Entrance Examination.

The Common Entrance Exams were designed to give a much broader percentage of the poorer class an opportunity to get a high school education. By and large it was a success. I, for one, would not have been able to attend high school had it not been for this system. Not withstanding, the exams were structured in such a way (unintentionally) that I believe favored the middle and upper class. Although students were tested in Reasoning, Logic and Mathematics, the bulk of the testing was in English. English is the official language of Jamaica. We are all educated in English, but, by and large, English is the language of the upper and middle class. Everyone in Jamaica understands and speaks the local vernacular – Patois; but it is mostly spoken by the poorer class. Patois is easiest described as broken English. While it may be English-based it, is interspersed with African, Arabic, French and Spanish words, reflecting the rich, diverse history of Jamaica and its people. The exams didn't really test how smart a child was. It was a very good gauge of how well you could learn by rote and regurgitate facts. If you studied the expected answers to the questions you could do well on the exams. According to the government, there is no "pass" or "fail," but rather those students with the highest scores are awarded the limited spaces in the high schools and, with the average school having only about 240 places (forty students in a class) each year, the competition was stiff.

It was every elementary school student's dream to pass the Common Entrance Examinations in the fifth or sixth grade. There were a few exceptional students who passed in the fourth grade, making it to high school at age ten. I believe that this was exactly the situation the system was trying to create; you could go as far as your abilities would take you. Passing these exams was an important milestone in the life of a child, and because failing brought with it such serious consequences, the burden and pressures to pass were tremendous. Failure meant that you had to attend a secondary school where more vocational subjects were taught and you had to live with appearing as a less than capable student. Of course, this perception is not true. My best friend in elementary school, Clive Reid, did not pass and he was a very smart guy. I am not sure what percentage of students is awarded a place in high school. The year I passed, fourteen students from my elementary school were awarded a place in the various high schools around Kingston, although more than 100 of us sat the exams. Success in the Common Entrance Exams meant that you would attend a high school where you would be placed on an academic track and at the end of school sit the General Certificate Examinations which, as I mentioned earlier, were set by the University of Cambridge or Oxford. On the strength of these passes you could go on to University or land a good job. My British peers at Sandhurst had the same academic qualifications as I got in Jamaica.

Of the two dozen or so high school aged children living on

my, street only three of us attended high school. The others attended a secondary school. I found myself spending more and more time at school hanging out with my friends. In fact, school became a haven for me. From the time I was in the ninth grade until I graduated from the thirteenth grade, I was in school six days a week. There was always something to do – running track, French club, quiz team, or just studying.

The people you choose to hang out with dictate the environment in which you find yourself every day. The people you closely associate with eventually determine the kinds of places in which you spend your time, but more importantly, the level of thinking and the kinds of influences that you expose yourself to. In the end, you will have to decide if your teammates are providing the guidance that supports the goals you are pursuing. Are they lifting you up and pushing you forward, or are they dragging you down and pulling you back?

Doctor Benjamin Carson grew up in Detroit, where he was raised by a single mother who only had a third grade education. In 1984, Doctor Carson was appointed the Director of Pediatric Neurosurgery at the John Hopkins Hospital in Baltimore. At thirty-three years old, he was the youngest person in the nation to have been appointed to such a position. He rose to prominence in 1987 when he led a team at the John Hopkins Hospital in Baltimore to separate a pair of seven-month-old German Siamese twins. The twins were joined at the head, and the surgery was especially risky because they shared a vital structure. This was the first time such a surgery was performed and both twins survived. In an interview I watched back in 1996 on the ABC program *Like It Is*, Gil Noble asked Carson how he would advise a young man who is subjected to negative peer pressure. Carson responded that, "The company you keep is the company you keep." He went on to say that you can always choose to hang out with the cool crowd but, "That company stays with you and it doesn't magically change one day. So you have to open your eyes and make your determination where most people who are 'cool' end up and ask yourself, is that where you want to be."

If your current teammates are supporting you, then you need to become like a sponge, soaking up as much as you can and of course give as much of yourself as well. If you are not getting the kind of support you need, then you need to remove yourself from the group. You would be surprised to know how much you can accomplish when you let go or at least minimize the time spent in negative, dead-end relationships. Successful people only hang around people who are headed in the same direction.

From where we lived on Sunrise Drive in Olympic Gardens, we had a clear view of Forest Hills about five miles away. Forest Hills was lined with big, beautiful mansions. Oftentimes, when I went for runs, I passed many of them with their well- manicured lawns and expensive cars parked in the driveway. Looking up on Forest Hills from Olympic Gardens, for me, was a constant reminder of that which I didn't have but it also gave me something to aspire to. Undoubtedly we lived in a depressed environment, but looking up on Forest Hills made me hopeful that things would change for the better. Hope is the lifeblood of possibility. On the other hand, for my peers who were from the old neighborhood, Forest Hills mansions told them that they were stuck in Olympic Gardens. That they were condemned to a life of lack and poverty. It reinforced in their minds that they were "sufferers".

By the time I was fifteen years old, it became clear to me that they and I were not heading in the same direction. Unlike them, I refused to see myself as a sufferer. That was a burden too heavy to bear, so I dropped them from my team. I didn't have anyone to advise or mentor me. I just knew that that their attitudes were not supportive of the goals I had established for myself, so getting them off my team was the right thing to do. It was around that time that I started running track and spending more time in school.

You may not be able to change the people around you, but you can certainly change the people you are around. You have to associate yourself with people who have a positive direction in their life and stay away from the negative ones. If you have to spend time with negative people, especially family and friends, as much as is possible, do it over the phone; but above all, do not discuss your goals and dreams with them. And what do you do, if you do not currently have in your life the kinds of people who can push and inspire you to greater heights? Let me suggest regular trips to your local library and bookstore. There, you will find people from all walks of life. People who have faced and overcome every single obstacle you could ever imagine. They have detailed their stories and provided you with personal advice. They would be more than happy to team up with you, get on your sled and help you to achieve your dreams as well.

CHAPTER 23

Have an Unwavering Vision

"To the person who does not know where he wants to go there is no favorable wind."

Seneca - Roman Philosopher and Statesman

When you have an idea to create something that is entirely new – a new product, service, business or any other belief or concept – more often than not you will discover that your biggest challenge is not believing that you can accomplish it, but convincing others to believe it. In 1988, people were shocked, and understandably so, to hear that Jamaica had started a bobsled team. In the beginning no one took us seriously. In many quarters we were seen as a media stunt, an amusing sideshow to the serious business of Olympic bobsledding. Even today, after so many years and significant accomplishments in the sport, people still crack up when they recall the first time they heard about our team. Their stereotypical view of Jamaica led them to believe that it was impossible for us to master the art of bobsledding, let alone become Olympic contenders. But that was their view. Ours was decidedly different. We saw ourselves as equals, as true competitors. We saw ourselves as athletes with the talent and the ability to become world class bobsledders. We had a vision of ourselves marching in that opening ceremony and having an opportunity to give of our best against the best.

Without vision the people perish. You start from where you are and climb on the strength of your vision to create the future you desire. Without a clear understanding of where you are going you will forever find yourself in an unending loop of mediocrity, dazed and confused as to why you are unable to reach your full potential. This is true personally and professionally. It is true for the Mom-and-Pop store as well as the large corporation.

Once you have decided what the direction is, once you have established where you want to be at some future date, you then surround yourself with the teammates who will give you the guidance and support and lend their perspective to you fulfilling that vision. Remember also that resumes aren't everything. You can always find someone with more degrees than a thermometer and a lifetime of experience that you can call on for help. However, if they don't believe in you and in what you are seeking to achieve, it will turn out be one big waste of time. It is well known that Jamaica has one of the most talented pools of sprinters in the entire world. George Fitch and William Maloney thought that finding the talent to breathe life into their bobsled idea would have been a slam dunk. As it turned out, they were unable to convince any of the summer athletes to cooperate.

As individual athletes we probably were not as gifted as the talent in the pool on our summer team. We all harbored Olympic aspirations, but given the paths we were on, at the time it is highly unlikely that any of us would have realized our Olympic ambitions. However, the minute we bought into the concept of the team we were able to succeed way beyond what any of us could have done on our own. This was a particular poignant lesson for me because, years before, I made the decision that I could succeed in sports without the help of teammates. My first love in sport was soccer. When it came time to tryout for the school team I couldn't because I didn't have soccer cleats. I used to play barefoot. Moreover, I hated the fact that I could lose a game because I had a teammate who didn't play his heart out. Track and field was different. I could run barefooted. I didn't need to own track spikes to be on the team, and more importantly, no one else was responsible for how well I ran. I dedicated myself to train as hard as I could and ride this train all the way to the Olympics. As it turned out, it was a team sport that took me to the Games. I know for a fact that I didn't have the speed to be an Olympic champion, nor did I have the endurance to be a middle distance threat on the world stage. In fact, none of us on the team had the total package to be an individual standout in world class competition. However, in pooling our individual talents and strengths and putting them behind a bobsled, we were able to achieve what none of us could have done on our own. Teamwork combines the abilities of the individuals into a power that becomes greater than the sum of its parts. The power that is generated through the cooperation of others becomes the spark that creates defining moments in our lives. It creates breakthroughs that become the hallmark of successful careers or business as well as provides us with lasting significance in our lives.

(CHAPTER 24)

Together Everyone Achieves More

"Alone we can do so little; together we can do so much."
Helen Keller -
American Author, Political Activist and Lecturer

I learned about the power of teamwork the hard way. As I mentioned earlier, I preferred track over soccer because I surmised that I didn't have to depend on anyone else to succeed. My high school did not retain a track coach for my second year in the sport. Building on the things I learned from the coach the previous season, I read books on middle distance running and designed my own training program. Our school library had a few books, but the one I liked best was one I discovered in a local bookstore. I didn't have the money to purchase it, so I used to make repeated trips to the store to read it. After a while, I caught the attention of the security guard. He noticed that I was frequently in the store dodging behind the shelves and assumed that I was shoplifting. He told me not to come back there. I was forced to save my lunch money and buy the book. It contained a wealth of information and was very helpful to me. From it I learned about many of the great middle distance runners –

Roger Bannister of Great Britain and the Flying Finns, Hannes Kolehmainen and Paavo Nurmi. The twelve Olympic Medals Nurmi won in track and field is unmatched by anyone else, and as a result he is often considered the greatest track and field athlete of all time. I also learned about *Fartlek* training. Fartlek is a Swedish word which means "speed play." This training method was developed in the 1930s by the Swedish coach Gustaf Holmér in an effort to improve the performance of the Swedish cross-country teams, which were dominated by Paavo Nurmi and the other Flying Finns in the 1920s. His idea was for the athletes to run faster than race pace while simultaneously concentrating on speed and endurance training. His concept worked so well that it was adopted by physiologists and coaches around the world, including me. I even devised some training exercises of my own. I used to, among other types of explosive exercises, hop on one leg from goal post to goal post on a soccer field, switch legs and go again. I didn't know it then, but those were not the kind of exercises a middle distance runner should have been doing. If I had a coach I would have known that. All in all, it appeared that I was inadvertently preparing for my bobsledding days.

By season's end, my name was circulating around Kingston as one of the guys to watch out for at Boys Champs. I believe that if I had a coach I would have performed much better at that meet. When I thought I had fallen far behind in that 800m race, the only thing I heard in my mind was the technical details and theories I had read in the book. It wasn't a coach's reassuring voice to **Keep On Pushing** even if it seemed as if the other guys had surged ahead. And with no coach's encouraging arm around me after my colossal failure and a nagging hamstring injury, I wallowed in self pity for the rest of my high school days. Although I still dominated the track within my high school, I never trained hard enough to be a threat on the national stage again.

Throughout your life, you will always find it helpful to have a coach or mentor to guide you along. It doesn't have to be a formal relationship. Surprisingly, despite my experience in high school, most of my mentors are the authors of books I have read. However, I recognize that that is not enough. I know I need to tap into the experience and wisdom of people who are operating in the real world and with whom I can interact with in real time; as a result, I pay close attention, especially to people whom I believe know more and are more experienced than I am in a particular area. Mentors, for the most part, provide invaluable help and advice. Nonetheless, in the final analysis, you have to decide whether or not accepting that advice is going to help you achieve your goal. It is still within your prerogative to accept or decline the advice. You may remember that I chose not to take Sam Bock's advice to give up on my dream of competing in the Nagano Olympics in 1998.

As I mentioned earlier, my quest to compete in the Nagano Games took me to the small town of Evanston, Wyoming. Because of the press we generated, a young man called Nigel Swaby, who lived in Salt Lake City, heard about us and wrote to me. He described himself as a businessman who would like to help us raise funds. Nigel was born in Jamaica to a Jamaican father and an American mother.

Additionally, something told me that Nigel was not as experienced as his letter suggested, and despite the invaluable help I was getting from my new teammates in Evanston, it was clear to me that I still needed some fresh ideas and energy. I figured that Nigel could provide a fresh set of lenses to look at our problems and had some contacts or at least make some contacts that our team wasn't able to make at the time, so I engaged him. I believe people should be given a chance to prove themselves. We all need those opportunities and we should provide them when we can.

During the early stages of working with Nigel, Paul Skog (the local attorney who invited us to Evanston), for reasons I don't remember now, got upset with him and strongly advised me not to work with him. I believed Paul's assessment to be sincere, but I did not take his advice. Nigel confided in me sometime afterwards that he thought I was going to fire him but, again, I think people should be given a chance to prove themselves, especially when you have nothing to lose and everything to gain.

About six weeks later, Nigel met Paul Bruno. Pablo, as I call him, was a marketing professional from Salt Lake City. Through his knowledge and contacts, he was able to pull together some resources that allowed us to continue training and, as I mentioned earlier, just weeks before the Olympics put together a sponsorship deal with one of his clients, a telecommunications company in Salt Lake City. No one person knows or can do everything. When you combine the skills of different people you are able to come up with different strategies, an improved product or a better outcome. As they say, the word **TEAM** is an acronym that stands for **T**ogether **E**veryone **A**chieves **M**ore.

BUILDING RELATIONSHIPS

Whether you want to accept it or not, we are all team players. Some of us are good team players, while some have chosen not to be. Our importance and the impact we are able to make during our lifetimes come from the quality of the relationships we foster. Of course, family life is the most fundamental of our team experiences. Other team experiences include our careers, civic organizations, religious groups, alumni associations and so on. Each of these teams represents an opportunity and provides a stage for us to live out our lives, pursue our hearts' desires and contribute to something beyond ourselves. When we give of ourselves and pour our hearts into these entities and join our efforts with those of our teammates, we become capable of achieving far more than we could have done working on our own. When the team grows, we grow. When the team succeeds, we succeed as well.

While the concept of teamwork is simple, like anything else in life, working successfully as a team is not always easy to achieve. There is no magic bullet. Teamwork doesn't fall in place simply because of ambition and desire, nor does it flourish just because the team enjoys an abundance of talent and skill. Successful teamwork comes from having solid relationships. People have to like being on the team. The more they enjoy working with their teammates, the harder they work and the quicker they will resolve inevitable conflicts and push towards achieving the team goals. Our team did not make it to Calgary without conflict. As you know, Sammy and I butted heads several times. He also had issues with the three soldiers on our team. He interpreted our demands for him to work harder and to be more focused as us ganging up on him because he was the lone civilian on the team. In the end, he left the team before we got to the Olympics. There were a number of fireworks between Pat Brown and the four of us. In the early days Pat played the role of administrator as well as coach in Howard Siler's absence. He still plays an important role in the life of the team to this day.

A sports team can have the most talented players in the league, but if even one of them does not feel good about being on the team, then they stand very little chance of winning the championship. Conflict between one or more members of a team isn't restricted to just them. The toxicity between the feuding parties spreads throughout and eventually consumes the entire team, thus adversely affecting performance. How many times have you seen a professional sports team struggle because of some kind of friction in the locker room only to see them soar the next season because a player is traded or the conflict is resolved in some other way? The same rings true in the board room, the emergency room or on the factory floor. In business, there are a few who somehow believe that the people side of business has very little to do with making money. However, the best business leaders know that profit and loss results are directly tied to the way people feel about the organization. To them, people's attitudes can work for or against them. Continued success on any level requires you to evaluate the relationships with your teammates.

Is everyone still working towards the same vision?

Is the team's vision still compatible with their personal goals?

Are they still motivated to achieve?

Are they growing and willing to adapt to the changing environment?

Finding out the answers to those questions will go a long way to make your team stronger by allowing you to work interdependently as, over time, you build faith and trust in each other. Human beings push and inspire each other as they work in this fashion.

COMPETITION DOES NOT HAVE TO EXCLUDE COOPERATION

Choose the sport, any sport, and you will find that there are only a few spots available on the team. At the beginning of the season there is a huge squad. Everyone is put through the paces, but, at the end of the day, everyone knows that not all of them will get a spot on the roster. Throughout this entire period the competition is fierce. Every athlete is pushing to out-perform the other. However, despite the competitive spirit of training camp, there is a strong spirit of cooperation that swirls among the athletes. They are fighting for a spot on the team but, at the same time, they are pushing, inspiring and helping each other to get better. Life is neither a sports team nor an athletic tournament. Success isn't reserved for the precious few. By employing the right strategies, every one of us has the ability to accomplish the things that we set out to do. Of course, in some ways our society suggests that this is not the case. There may only be a few job openings in a particular company and, as they say, "May the best man win!" The fierce competition, especially in an economic downturn, has certainly created a "dog-eat-dog" world. I don't believe it has to be this way, though. We do not have to adopt the "all or nothing" approach to our challenges. When we **Keep On Pushing**, especially during times of crisis, we leave ourselves open to opportunities we may not have noticed or even considered before. As a result, we are able to enlist the help of others, including our former competitors, in order to get to that next level.

COLLABORATION LEADS TO CONTRIBUTION

We all have benefited from teamwork. We have benefited directly from those who have nurtured and mentored us, but just as important is that fact that we have benefitted indirectly from those who have counseled our mentors. I believe that success, however you may define it, and even if you would say that you are not anywhere near the success you would like to achieve, should foster benevolence and philanthropy. When we intelligently give of ourselves – when we share time, information, earnings and so on – we improve the lives of others and, in the process improve, ourselves as well. Shakespeare said, "The scent of a rose lingers on the hand that casts it." In other words, you cannot lift up or encourage someone without doing the same for yourself. Everyone wins through teamwork. And after all, isn't becoming, doing and having more what it is all about?

KEY POINTS TO REMEMBER - LESSON 8

- Nothing of significance was ever achieved by one person acting by themselves. Teams come in all shapes and sizes and serve different purposes. Your first teammates were your parents who loved and nurtured you during those early years. Other important teammates include teachers and mentors who provide guidance and support, friends who meet social needs, coworkers who help you to grow professionally and very close friends in whom you can confide.

- The richness and quality of your life is in no small part due to the quality of the teammates you have chosen and the quality of the relationships you have developed with them. You would be surprised to know how much you can accomplish when you let go of or at least minimize the time you spend around dead end relationships.

- More often than not you will discover that your biggest challenge is not believing that you can accomplish a goal but convincing others to believe that it is possible and soliciting their help. As an individual, if you foster good will with enough people you will get help to accomplish almost any goal you desire.

ASSIGNMENTS

1. Take great care in choosing the people you spend most of your time with.

2. Seek out mentors and coaches. If you don't personally know anyone who might be suitable, you can always find mentors on the shelves of your local library and bookstore.

3. Get in the habit of giving of yourself and encouraging others.

Speaking at an incentive meeting for a fortune 500 company in Montego Bay, Jamaica.

Meeting kids at the track during the Olympics in Nagano 1998.

Winning Is Not Always About the Final Score

*"Let me win but if I cannot win,
let me be brave in the attempt."*
Special Olympics Motto

W atching four big guys sprinting at top speed down the hill and then loading into a tiny sled is almost like watching the delicate, well-choreographed movements of a dance recital. Aggression, brute force and speed are balanced by teamwork, coordination and precision. Our team had mastered the first half of the equation. The hours of pushing the makeshift sled on the Army base in Kingston had served us well, but we still had a long way to go in learning how to look like ballerinas on ice. I rode in the second seat behind Dudley, followed by Michael and Chris. On our second run, Michael's spikes got stuck in my thighs and it took me a while to dislodge them and guide his feet to his foot pegs in the sled. As we slid through corner two, I could hear the spectators shouting, "sit down! sit down!" To them, it seemed as if Michael was planning to ride all the way down the track standing, although all this time we were fighting frantically to guide his feet through the tight spaces between my thighs and the sides of the sled so that he could sit. By the end of the corner we were able to take their advice.

On the second day of the race we were hopeful and determined to turn in a better performance. We followed our normal routine. After breakfast, we caught the coach out to the track. Michael, Chris and I loaded the sled on the truck and took it to the top while Dudley went off to walk the track. By the time we were done putting on the runners, polishing down the sled again and making sure the driving ropes were not entangled, we still had another hour or so before the race started. We were just hanging around in the warm-house when Dudley returned from his track walk. He wore a miserable, dejected look. It turned out that during his walk he had slipped and fell on the ice and sprained his collar bone. Roy, the physiotherapist from Great Britain, applied some magic spray and we were good to go again.

I didn't find out until about a year later, but as we stood on the starting blocks waiting on the officials to clear the track for us, George Fitch came up to Dudley and told him that our coach, Howard Siler, had left the Olympics. He had to return to work and George came to vent his frustrations to Dudley just as he was about to embark on the biggest race of his life. Certainly that was a distraction for Dudley. The other guys and I were oblivious to this. We were just raring to go. The track cleared, we got on the blocks and ended up pushing the seventh fastest start time of the day. The loading of the sled was smooth – ballerina on ice. We settled down in the sled and were enjoying the ride. We hit the wall as we exited corner eight, but there is a long straightway before corner nine so I was not concerned. I figured we had enough time to correct the sled for a smooth entrance onto nine. However, just before we got onto corner nine, we hit the wall again. This time I knew the transition was not going to be so smooth. Corner nine was the kreisel - a long left hand turn.

Instead of following a smooth line all the way around, I expected the sled to go high up on the turn, wave a little and then bang really hard on the left wall as it exited the corner. It would have been a bumpy, painful ride but we would have been on all fours still heading down the track. The next thing I knew, my head was slamming on the ice. In watching the tape, I realized that we were simply too high on the end of the corner. At the point where the sled should have been going down we were actually coming up and there was just nowhere for the sled to go but over. It was a very spectacular crash. So spectacular, in fact, that Hollywood could not find a stunt man crazy enough to duplicate it. In *Cool Runnings* they suggested that the crash occurred because of a loose nut on the sled. Those guys have a very vivid imagination. The only loose nut we had was George complaining to Dudley about the coach at the start of the race.

CHAPTER 25

Learn And Grow From Your Experiences

"Be brave. Take risks. Nothing can substitute experience."
Paulo Coelho -
Brazilian Lyricist and Novelist

You would think that if I was in a bobsled and it flipped over as spectacularly as we did in Calgary going at almost 80 mph, I would have been concerned for my life. That was the furthest thing from my mind. That crash in Calgary happened to be my seventh for the season and while you never ever get comfortable or take a crash for granted, I was not thinking about the fact that I could have lost my life. I have always been worried about crashing in a four-man sled. Since a four-man sled is so cramped, I was concerned that I might feel claustrophobic or at least get wedged in a position such that I would be unable to move as my head got slammed into the wall. On that day, however, those things were furthest from my mind. As I skated on my head – survival instincts in full gear – the only thing I felt was embarrassment. The entire world was watching and we failed miserably. Our detractors must have been having a field day. My next thoughts were about how we were going to go back home to Jamaica. Jamaica has such high expectations of its athletes and is not shy about letting you know when you have not measured up. What will we say? How will we ever be able to hold our heads high? What could we possibly do to make up for this?

The sled finally came to a stop after we skated on our heads for what felt like an eternity. When we crawled out, it became clear that we had not crossed the finish line and so the Olympics were over for us. Even if we had broken the timing eyes and got a finish time, in a race that is decided by hundredths of a second, we would have still ended up a distant last place.

The walk down the braking stretch was long and painful. We felt like complete failures, humiliated, and found ourselves doing the difficult dance of trying to get off the track and out of the limelight quickly and gracefully. As we walked down the braking stretch, a curious thing began to take place. The spectators began to cheer and shout, "We love you!" One guy reached over to shake my hand and others followed suit. The outpour was spontaneous and genuine and softened the sting of the embarrassment I felt. I finished the walk shaking hands, waving at the crowds and smiling.

Of course, we still had a problem. How were we going to face our countrymen back home? Embarrassing a nation that had become known around the world for its sporting excellence certainly meant that we would be greeted with ridicule and jeers. We resigned ourselves to facing the music, but here again we were surprised. We were given a hero's welcome, and the government even put out some stamps with our images on it. That certainly gave new meaning to the term "personal mail." I would get letters and the stamp on it would have my face! I often joke that I would look at those letters and think, "What a handsome devil."

Sports are a great metaphor for life. The ebb and flow of a sporting competition is, in many ways, reminiscent of life's daily challenges. Participating in sports requires you to challenge yourself and invest time to develop your physical abilities, and prepares you to test those abilities against other athletes. A personal desire to do well, meet the expectations of parents, coaches, your hometown or even an entire nation, as well as the importance of the particular competition all combine to create an enormous pressure to succeed. The same is true in life. Most of us spend several years in school developing our academic abilities and challenging ourselves in order to be able to jump into the job market or business world, all the while dealing with the pressure that comes from the high expectations of parents and teachers, as well as our own personal desire to make it. The discipline and teamwork that are so necessary for success in sports are equally important for success in life. The thrill and satisfaction that come over you from winning even a simple pick-up game can be easily equated to the sense of accomplishment one feels after achieving even minor goals.

Losing a championship game is painful. Have you ever studied the faces of the guys on the bench of the losing team? These guys are paid millions of dollars to play sports, and yet many of them are brought to tears because they didn't win a trophy they could easily buy with money they may have squandered in an evening. Failing to achieve an important goal is just as painful. As in the case of the athlete, success for most people is not just about the prize at the end; it is also about the investment of time, energy and emotion. It is about passion and commitment and a belief that your efforts will yield the results you seek. When you invest yourself so heavily into something, it is only natural that you fully expect to get what you set out to achieve. In a sporting event there is going to be a loser. Even when two athletes cross the finish line with the same exact time, the winner is chosen from a photo. It is a harsh reality because the final results are just that – final. Although the scoreboard is the final arbiter, the story it tells is not complete. It does not tell how well the losing team played. Neither does it reflect the enormous obstacles the losing team may have had to overcome just to make it that far in the competition, nor the amazing way they worked as a team, nor how much they have improved, how hard they fought.

Sometimes during my presentations I would ask how many of my audience members remember watching the four-man event in Calgary. Usually a fair number would put their hands up. Whenever I ask if they remember who the medal winners were, invariably nobody does. But they all remember the Jamaican bobsled team. For the record, the Swiss won that race by seven hundredths of a second over the East Germans, and on the final run the Soviet Union team squeaked by the Americans in one hundredth of a second for the bronze. I suspect that people are more inclined to remember our team, as opposed to the medal winners, not simply because of how amusing or unusual it was for a group of guys from the tropics to compete in the Winter Olympic Games. I think their love affair with the Jamaica bobsled team reflects the fact that they admire and can relate to us in a way that they cannot relate to any of the traditional teams in the sport. This is by no means meant to be a knock on any of those teams. I believe that they are respected for the high level at which they compete. These teams are always expected to contend for a medal. However, in us, people saw audacity, courage and determination – qualities they themselves need to have in order to pursue the dreams that they have put on hold for so long. To them it didn't matter if we won. What was more important was the fact that we had the temerity to even stand up and try.

You might never fail as spectacularly as we did on that bright but cold February afternoon in Calgary, with so many eyewitnesses around the world. But some failure in life is unavoidable.

Unless you live your life so cautiously and guarded that you might as well not have lived at all, which in my mind is failure by default, it is impossible to live without failing. Imagine that we had won the gold medal in Calgary. What a wonderful fairy tale ending that would have been! I am not going to lie and say I didn't want to win the race. What would be the point of being in the race in the first place? Even the biggest underdog with all the odds stacked against him is trying with all his might to pull off an upset. Had we become Olympic Champions that year we would have become true overnight successes. It would have been a real fairy tale, but as you know, life is no fairy tale. If we had won that race the message and the lesson from the experience would have been that you can still achieve amazing things without paying the price. There is no doubt that we worked incredibly hard to get to Calgary. In fact, you could easily argue that our lifetime of training and competing in sports, coupled with a few months of focused, intense preparations as bobsledders, helped us to reach one of the recognized pinnacles of the sporting world – the Olympic Games. However, it required a lot more than what we did to reach the very summit – Olympic Gold medalist.

That crash has given me more than any medal could have. As former Supreme Court Justice Oliver Wendell Holmes Jr. once wrote, "A mind that is stretched by a new experience can never go back to its old dimensions." The experience has taught me unequivocally that through hard work, focus, commitment, a positive, never-say-die attitude and belief in yourself, you can make impossible dreams come true. If you frame your failures correctly, you should emerge from the experience wiser, stronger and secure with the knowledge that you have the ability to survive anything that life throws at you. It doesn't make future pursuits any easier, but it gives you the knowledge and the assurance that you have the strength and courage to pursue something new and difficult and still have a reasonable chance of succeeding.

As I mentioned earlier, every competitive person wants very much to win. That is why they prepare so thoroughly and compete so fiercely. I can attest to the fact that not winning is incredibly disappointing. The sting of defeat hurts, and we live in a culture that adores winners. I often speak at incentive meetings where the top sales people, along with their spouses, are wined and dined in exotic locations around the world. What does it say about those who were not invited on the trip? Does it mean that they are losers? I believe it is important to resist the tendency to measure success purely in terms of results.

I admit that this is a very difficult thing to do, especially in the business world, where success is judged by money, profits, status and rank. During these tough economic times, companies are hyper-focused on the bottom line. While nothing is wrong with that, it is important to note that the final outcomes are usually a result of the systems and processes that are in place. Money and profits are by products of mastering those systems and processes. It is a lot like me telling my driver Sammy to focus on learning how to steer the sled along the fastest paths of the corners. Improving on that skill would undoubtedly improve our finish times. As real estate developer Donald Trump said, "I don't make deals for the money. I've got enough, much more than I'll ever need. I do it to do it. Other people paint beautifully on canvas or write wonderful poetry. I like making deals, preferably big deals. That's how I get my kicks."

If you set your goals correctly you should have a 50/50 chance of achieving them. In other words, the chances of you not hitting your mark are just as great as you making it to the proverbial mountain top. If it so happens that you did not quite hit your goal, does it mean that the entire effort was a complete failure? I do not think so! You may not have hit the mother lode, but are you further along the road than you were yesterday? Do you know more about what needs to be done than when you first started out? What old skills have you strengthened and polished? What new ones have you learned? Although you did not quite hit your mark, would it be fair to say that you are a better person, practicing more empowering habits than you were a month ago, six months ago or even a year ago? You have to be willing to say to yourself, "I am on the right path. I am doing fine. I am making progress."

CHAPTER 26

Pursue Your Own Definition of Success

"If your success is not on your own terms, if it looks good to the world but does not feel good in your heart, it is not success at all."
Anna Quindlen -
Journalist, Author and Opinion Columnist

At some point in our lives we live according to what the world defines success to be. Perhaps in one sense, at the outset, we needed the guidance of people in our lives to understand what success is. In the end, however, it is still your life and ultimately you will have to decide what success means to you. You can never live up to the world's definition of success, but you can easily meet yours. We all watched the scintillating performance of the Jamaican track team at the Beijing Olympics. Usain Bolt was particularly dominating, slowing up ten meters before the finish line to celebrate his victory in the 100m event. Many people questioned why did he didn't run all out to the finish line. They wanted to see him lower his own world record. Bolt's performance was arguably the most dominating in the history of the Olympics, but people wanted more. To Bolt's credit, his response was, "My aim was to be the Olympic champion and I did just that, so I'm happy with myself."

No one can define success for you. You get to choose and pay the price in terms of effort and sacrifice as well as hours, days, months and years you invest in it. Our team didn't dominate in Calgary the way Usain Bolt did in Beijing. In fact, we suffered one of the most spectacular crashes in the history of Olympic bobsledding. It was a colossal failure, but in just a few short months we had transformed ourselves from a middle distance runner, a soccer player and two aspiring sprinters who knew nothing about the sport to Olympic bobsledders. I admit that I might be biased. But it is difficult for me not to see that as successful.

We all have our own unique sets of skills and experience. It is foolhardy to compare yourself to others and to beat yourself up if you fall short. Like our team, you might find yourself going up against someone who, at that point in time, knows a lot more and has far more experience and resources than you do. The fact that you had to overcome so many more challenges than they did just to have your name considered for the promotion means that you have succeeded. Even if you have stumbled along the way, the fact that you had to endure and overcome so much more just to be in the game means that you have succeeded immensely.

Who doesn't want to stand on the podium and hear the cheers of others? Who doesn't want to see their name in lights? It is great to be the on the honor roll, or to be recognized as the employee of the month or sales person of the year, but if in all your endeavors you gave it your all and can look back with no regret about the effort that you put in, then you've succeeded. The dyslexic child who learned to read at grade level should not be down on himself because he isn't the valedictorian. A social introvert who builds herself up to become one of the top salespersons in the company should not feel badly for not being named salesperson of the year. Just look at what they had to overcome.

As famed Olympian Jesse Owens once said, "Success is to be measured not so much by the position that one has reached in life as by the obstacles which he has overcome while trying to succeed." In suggesting that you start to measure your level of success not simply by a destination at which you have arrived but rather an objective evaluation of your journey is not to encourage an acceptance of mediocrity. Mediocrity comes about when we become contented with below average performances. Our team was never contented with its performance in the Calgary Olympics. Highly successful people are never satisfied when they miss their goals. Having said that, I believe that we can choose to look at our failures in a way that is fresh and healthy and does not lead us down the path of mediocrity. We have become quite adept at pointing out our flaws and highlighting our failures. We also need to become equally adept at identifying our strengths, becoming aware of our growth and recognizing our achievements as well.

When we define success according to how the world at large defines it, we constantly find ourselves looking at our accomplishments in relation to others, instead of in relation to our full potential. Sports are as much about competing against your opponent as they are about competing against yourself. Getting the upper hand over an opponent is great. It is a wonderful ego boost to be declared the champion. What is not so glamorous, but infinitely better, is competing against yourself and getting the most out of your abilities and talents. I have discovered that when you strive to be the best that you can be you not only grow, sometime by leaps and bounds, but, in the process, you inspire others to do the same as well.

CHAPTER 27

Inspire Others To Be Their Best

"Learn and grow all you can; serve and befriend all you can; enrich and inspire all you can."
William Arthur Ward - Author

When he ascended to the peak on May 25, 2001, Erik Weihenmeyer became the first and only blind person to have ever climbed Mount Everest. Climbing Mount Everest is an incredible achievement. Many have been rebuffed by the mountain numerous times. Currently, there are approximately 120 bodies frozen in the ice on the mountain. Those who have made it to the top describe an amazing challenge that pushed them to their very limits. Getting to the top of the highest point on earth is a phenomenal feat, but, in my opinion, a hundred times more so when accomplished by a blind person. Yet, despite our memorable exit from the 1988 Olympics, Erik said he was inspired by us. It is sobering and flattering to be watching a young girl, an amputee, remarking that if four guys from Jamaica can become Olympic bobsledders, then she can be a world class sprinter; or to meet a group of young girls from Atlanta who call their soccer team the *Cool Runners* because they were inspired by the Disney blockbuster movie about us. Over the years I have met countless people from many parts of the world, some of them barely able to speak English, who have told me that we inspired them or somebody they knew to pursue their dreams.

Our society respects and admires high achievers. Because their accomplishments fall so far outside of the norm they are almost seen as super humans, and the average person, despite the fact that they have similar capabilities, does not feel like they can climb to such dizzying heights. I believe there is a greater good to overcoming insurmountable odds and still falling short of your goal. It inspires others. It makes you look human and allows others to empathize and relate to you. They see you as someone plagued with the same human weaknesses as they are, and surmise that if you had the courage to go after such audacious dreams then they can summon the temerity to go after theirs as well. They figure, "If he can do it, so can I." Despite our spectacular crash and ultimate failure to complete the third run at the Calgary Olympics, our team discovered that you just never know who you might move to pursue the dreams they had on hold or were reluctant to pursue because of fear. I have met enough people from around the world to convince me that this is true. We didn't stand on the medal podium, but off the track we walked away as huge winners.

KEY POINTS TO REMEMBER - LESSON 9

- Unless you live your life so cautiously and guarded that you might as well not have lived at all, it is impossible to live without failing.

- If you frame your failures correctly, you should emerge from the event wiser, stronger and secure with the knowledge that you have the ability to survive.

- You can never live up to the world's definition of success but you can meet yours, so you should endeavor to live your life based only on your definition of success. When you define success according to how the world at large defines it, you constantly find ourselves looking at your accomplishments in relation to your full potential.

- Resist the temptation to compare yourself to others and to beat yourself up if you fall short. At this point in your life, you just might not have the experience and resources that others do. Choose to focus only on your own unique sets of abilities, skills and knowledge.

ASSIGNMENTS

1. Get in the habit of identifying and celebrating the things you have done right and the small successes you have achieved while working towards a bigger goal.

2. Enjoy your success while you objectively examine how you can improve on the things that did not go as well as you would have liked.

Out Of Many, We All Are One

"We all should know that diversity makes for a rich tapestry, and we must understand that all the threads of the tapestry are equal in value no matter what their color."

Maya Angelou - American Poet

I magine that you could fly over an Olympic Games and zoom down at any given moment to take a snap shot. What would you see? From higher up you would see a beehive of activities made up of people who are short, tall, thin, broad, men, women, younger, older. You would see black, brown, yellow, white skin colors. You would see individuals from different nations and different ethnic groups. Some teams will be mono-ethnic, but if you zoom in tighter you will notice persons of different races on many national teams. But those would only be the obvious differences. Zoom in tighter still, right into their minds and lives. What would you see then? You would see individuals with different life experiences, perspectives and interests. You would see people with different political and religious beliefs and sexual orientations. You would see gender and generational differences. You would also see that they have all come together as individual threads intertwined in this rich tapestry known as the human race, all playing an important role in the greatest show on earth – the Olympic Games. As an athlete, I have had the good fortune of witnessing all of this in an intimate way, and I view the Olympic experience as truly a utopian one, where differences are acknowledged, embraced and celebrated.

Sports in general and the Olympics in particular have long recognized and accepted what other areas of society around the world are now embracing: The fact that neither your race, ethnic background, age or any other arbitrary norm or label can define the limits of your success or prevent you from exploring your full potential. I believe that all of us, without exception, have the ability to become that which we aspire to be. The only limitations are the ones we impose on ourselves through the limit of our imagination. This ability is innate in all of us. It is as much a part of the makeup of our DNA as the color of our eyes, the shape of our lips or our skin tone. Sports, more than any other segment of society, has demonstrated time and again that this ability and our desire for success far supersede the power of our outward characteristics to determine our level of success.

When kids play, the world wins: *Volunteering with fellow Right to Play athlete ambassadors in Sierra Leone, West Africa.*

People Are People

"Individually, we are one drop. Together, we are an ocean."
Ryunosuke Satoro - Japanese Poet

A few years ago, I was watching a promotional video that was produced by Right to Play, an athlete-driven, humanitarian organization which supports the right of children to play. As one of the many athlete ambassadors in the organization, I support sports and play programs in twenty-three countries around the world, including Africa, the Balkans, the Middle East, South America and Thailand. The tape I was watching was about a soccer program that was developed in the Middle East with Arab and Israeli boys. During his interview, the team's coach made the point that despite the political, religious, social, economic and security turmoil that these kids live in daily, it all seems to melt away when they are on the soccer field. Through the power of sports, they are able to see each other not through the prism of decades of hatred, mistrust and stark differences, but simply as another human being. He reiterated his point by saying "People are people." I could immediately identify with what he was saying.

The Calgary Olympic Games took place while the world was still fully engaged in the Cold War. That was one of areas of study we undertook while I was a cadet at the Royal Military Academy Sandhurst, so I was quite familiar with the prevailing attitudes. The Soviet Union and its satellite states in Eastern Europe were the sworn enemies of the West, and since my instructions were only from the point of view of the West I had the impression that everybody behind the Iron Curtain was evil. While in the Olympic Village, I finally came face to face with many of the representatives of these evil regimes. I watched them closely with their game faces on as they boarded the coaches to their respective competition venues. I observed them milling around the village, enjoying hamburgers and other foods on the decadent Western menu, playing video games in the games arcade and hanging out in the discotheque. It didn't take long for me to realize that the only real difference between us was ideology. Both of us – they and I – were athletes – people with a dream to represent our countries with pride and distinction at the Olympic Games. We shared the same hopes and aspirations, demonstrated the same level of commitment and dedication, and suffered from the same human frailties and short comings. We were more alike than we were different. Unlike the rest of society, on a whole, athletes recognize and accept this. Perhaps it is because we understand the investment required to earn the right to march in an Olympic Opening Ceremony and to hopefully have a piece of shiny metal hung around your neck. Not just for the sake of being able to claim that piece of metal, but for what it says about you as a person. You dared to dream and dared to pay the price in order to live that dream. That puts them, and anyone who makes that kind of commitment and sacrifice, regardless of their field of endeavor, in a special class and creates a bonding and a sense of brotherhood that goes beyond societal norms. On rare occasions you see this bond being displayed in the competitive arena.

In 1936, the world was on the verge of war. Nazism was bristling in Berlin with red and black swastikas flying everywhere. Hitler was using the Olympic Games as a stage to promote his propaganda of Aryan superiority. One of the underpinnings of Hitler's philosophy on the superiority of the Aryan race was that blacks were not only inferior, but that they were also sub-human.

Jesse Owens exposed the flaws in Hitler's argument by winning the 100m event over another African-American, Ralph Metcalfe. In the long jump, Owens almost fouled out after the officials counted one of his practice runs down the runway and into the pit as an attempt. Owens' strongest competitor in the event was a tall, blond, blue-eyed German named Luz Long. Long, who had had easily qualified for the finals, introduced himself to Owens and advised him on how to approach his final jump. Long deduced that Jesse could easily clear the minimum distance required for him to make the finals, so he suggested that Owens jumped from a spot several inches from the line. Owens took his advice and not only qualified for the finals but went on to beat Luz Long for the gold. Speaking about the courage it took for Luz long to befriend him in front of Adolf Hitler, Owens was quoted as saying, "You can melt down all the medals and cups I have and they wouldn't be a plating on the 24-karat friendship I felt for Luz Long at that moment."

Eugenio Monti was the preeminent bobsled driver in the world from 1957 through 1968. When I met him in St. Moritz, Switzerland in 1990, he was introduced to me as the greatest of all time. At the 1964 Games in Igls, Austria, Monti and his brakeman Sergio Siorpaes were the defending World Champions. They were locked in a heated competition with the British team of Anthony Nash and Robin Dixon. The Brits broke a bolt on their sled, which was sure to lead to their withdrawal from the race, but Monti loaned them a bolt from his sled and they went on to win the gold medal. In the four man event, the Canadians damaged their sled's axle and would have been disqualified, but once again Monti and his mechanics helped repair their sled and they took the gold medal in the race. Luz Long, Eugenio Monti and many other athletes like them demonstrate through their actions that they want to be crowned champion only if, on that day, their performance outclassed that of the competition, and not because they were of a certain hue, religion or political persuasion. In fact, the imposition of such labels, and the denial of someone to compete because they are different, waters down the competition and diminishes the accomplishments of those who were not subjected to those restrictions. They are willing to help their main rivals remain in the competition even if they are from a different country or a supposedly inferior race. Athletes know instinctively that those artificial labels do not determine someone's ability and serve no good purpose.

Most times this bonding and acceptance takes place far from the field of competition. Like the time I was in a restaurant in La Plagne, France with Jeff Woodard, an African-American from the Catskills, New York, and Aldis Intlers, a Latvian-born brake man on the Soviet Team. This was the first time Jeff and I were getting a chance to know him. We were struck by how smart and witty he was. He had us rolling on the floor as he described, in very broken English, his amusement the first time he saw me, a black bobsled driver, going through the visualization process in the warm house. We became very good friends after that and I was devastated when I learned of his tragic death in a car accident in his native Latvia.

Bobsledding is predominantly a white sport. During the time I competed, Dudley Stokes, Collin Harris (of Great Britain) and I were the only black drivers on the international circuit. All the other black athletes in the sport were brakemen and pushers, recruited mainly from track and field because of their explosive speed. Until Aldis Intlers pointed out how unusual it was for him to see a black bobsled driver, I didn't think anything of it. The world of sports is a fascinating one. You get to meet funny Latvians and black bobsled drivers.

Although sports, for the most part, look past the outward differences and accepts the athlete as just another human being, there is some amount of behavior that is influenced by a stereotypical view of race. I suppose that is inevitable since there are bound to be societal influences on sports. I personally don't believe such behaviors are meant to be insulting. Teams are always looking for anything that can give them a winning edge, and we sometimes buy into the stereotypical view that "white men can't jump" or "black men can't swim," and so on. Needless to say, these assumptions can be very wrong. The team from the United States Virgin Islands was all white and had excruciatingly slow start times. They were always impressed by our start times and how competitive they were. One year they turned up on the circuit with a lone black guy who was almost as slow as cold molasses. They seemed to have managed to find the slowest black guy in all of the Virgin Islands. We were all friends, so I often teased them about their new strategy and let them know that not every black guy can run fast.

The Calgary Olympic Games was an interesting experience for me as an athlete. I was there to compete and give my best for my country, and I was certainly dedicating my energies to that task. However, being so new in the sport, I spent a lot of time watching the other teams, tying to pick up a tip or two from them. Also, the Olympic Games were the first time I was seeing any of the big names in the sport. It is like making it to the NBA finals and seeing Julius Erving, Larry Bird or Michael Jordan for the first time, although you have been hearing of them since the day you first picked up a basketball. I suppose that is how the rest of the world felt at the Barcelona Olympics when the Dream Team arrived. There is a story about a player who asked one of his teammates on the bench to snap a picture of him guarding Magic Johnson. I remember being in the warm house looking around in awe. We had competed against most of the nations racing at the Olympics in the only World Cup race we did in Igls, Austria the November before. But those were the second tier teams from those nations. These guys were the big guns. You could see it in their swagger. They all had a very confident air about them. I was also amazed by the amount of equipment they had. We already knew that they had a lot more warm clothing than we did. The Olympic Games were the first time we really looked like a team after we had our speed suits presented to us on stage during a fundraiser at a restaurant in downtown Calgary. But these guys looked like they had a traveling workshop, while we only had a few nuts and bolts and an adjustable wrench. I was also trying to put a face to the names of the "who's who" of bobsled driving. While I sat there with my mouth wide open and starry eyed, one of the East German drivers, I suspect it was Wolfgang Hoppe, the world number one at the time, took a quick break from his race preparations, smiled at me and handed me an East German pin. This was no small gesture on his part. In those days, the East Germans and the Soviets were not allowed to interact with the other teams. They came, raced, packed up their gear, and left. That day, through his gesture, the East German was saying to me, "We belong to the fraternity of athletes. We are one."

I have had some great experiences in my life, but easily one of the best took place in Nagano, Japan in 1998. During the Games each team was asked to *adopt* a school. This is not a usual practice during the games. Of the three Olympics I've competed in, Nagano was the only time it happened. Our school was the Soosobanah Elementary School in Nagano. When a team enters the

Olympic Village, there is usually a welcoming ceremony. During the ceremony, your national flag is raised, your National Anthem played and the Mayor of the Olympic Village delivers a welcoming address. Students from the adoptive schools were present during the Welcoming Ceremonies in Nagano. What was different for us was that our National Anthem was not played. The students from the Soosobanah Elementary School sang ours. What was even more remarkable was the fact that they did not speak English. They had learned to sing the anthem phonetically. Afterwards, we cheered and hugged them to show our appreciation for the enormous courage it took to make such a gesture. A few days later we visited their school and it was an instant love fest. In all the years I have been bobsledding, I have never seen anyone so excited to meet us. They were dressed in black, green and gold jackets, and had little Jamaican flags waving. In true Japanese style, we traded our sneakers for slippers before we entered the auditorium, where the children taught us some traditional Japanese children's games and treated us to a number of performances. We ended our time there singing the song voted by the BBC as the song of the millennium; "One Love" by Bob Marley. On stage with the team members were reggae singing stars Freddy McGregor, Carlene Davis and Tommy Cohan and, of course, some of the students. As we were singing "let's get together and feel alright," Freddy McGregor rubbed the head of one of the boys who was standing right in front of me and in a very moving, sincere tone told him that the only thing that separated us was language. Freddy spoke in *patois*, the local vernacular in Jamaica, so the kid definitely didn't understand a word that was said to him – but he looked up on Freddy, his face sporting his strong Japanese features, and smiled as if he understood him perfectly. It was truly a moment of oneness. As that soccer coach from the Middle East said, "People are people."

CHAPTER 29

Patriotism Gives Way to Athleticism

"In everyone's life, at some time, our inner fire goes out. It is then burst into flame by an encounter with another human being."
Albert Schweitzer -
German-French Theologian, Musician and Philosopher

The Olympic Games are one of the few events in the world where everyone is treated as equals. Small, impoverished nations burst with as much pride as rich, powerful ones. A nation's GDP or military might has very little relevance in the competition arena. All that matters is how the athletes perform. The Games begin and end with a parade of nations, with each national team marching behind their national flags. In the field of competition, athletes are not only vying for personal accomplishments, they are attempting to bring glory to the country as well. However, despite this overwhelming surge of national pride, one of the things that make the Olympic Games such a special, heart-warming, truly memorable event is the shared joy and shared pride in human athletic prowess and achievement. Americans will express the same joy of watching Michael Phelps' phenomenal feat of winning eight gold medals as watching Usain Bolt burn up the track for Jamaica. The Canadians enjoy watching their hockey team capturing gold as much as they enjoy watching the Russian figure skaters humble the competition. Actually, that might be a stretch. Nothing comes between a Canadian and his hockey, but I am sure you get my drift. The bottom line is that, at the Olympics, great performances are appreciated and applauded regardless of race, ethnicity or national origin.

DIVERSITY MEANS EQUALITY FOR ALL

I grew up with the concept of equality for all. At least in theory. A 2006 estimate indicates the Jamaican population of 2.6 million people is made up of several different ethnic groups. 90.9% of Jamaicans are of West African descent – sons and daughters of former slaves. 7.3% are of mixed race; 1.3% are of East Indian heritage; 0.3 are white; 0.2% are Chinese; and 0.1% are classified as "Other." I attended high school with this ethnic mix without any racial tension whatsoever. You will never hear someone describing themselves as an African-Jamaican, Chinese-Jamaican, Jewish-Jamaican, or any other such nomenclature. We are all simply Jamaicans. Our multi-racial roots have given birth to one nation, hence our national motto, "Out of Many, One People." There is real racial harmony, but there is a clear distinction among the social classes. This disparity is not supported by the laws the way apartheid was in South Africa, but it is evident in attitudes. When you are born and raised in the ghetto, as I was, you are somehow made to feel that your options are limited. Again, in theory, this is not so. Everyone has equal access to education, and in theory can go as far as their abilities and desire will take them.

However, in practice, somehow the neighborhood in which you grow can determine the extent to which you succeed. If you grow up in the ghetto, ambition and hard work is not enough. You need someone with stature to vouch for you. In his song

"Rat Race," Bob Marley laments this sad state of affairs when he said, "But we no have no friends; In-a high society."

Sports were one of the first places that I found my voice. On the field, it didn't matter what was in your pocket. All that mattered was what was in your heart. Anyone who has ever played sports knows it as the great equalizer. Once the rules are adhered to, it gives no regard to race, class, religious background or any other labels. Sports level the playing field, and you are judged simply on the merits of your abilities and performance. That is what is so great about the Olympic Games. Everyone has an opportunity.

Whether you are in Africa or America, China or the Caribbean, society's tendency to view us through certain prisms, as well as the way we have been conditioned as a result of how society sees those perceived differences, necessitate that you have to reprogram how you feel about yourself if you hope to succeed. This is true of anyone; even Olympic athletes have had to reprogram how they feel about themselves. They have had to learn to see the unique qualities in themselves and not the stereotypical view that society has of them. Our team was decidedly different from any other team in the history of the Winter Olympics. Being the first team from a developing country in the tropics to compete in a sport that has it roots in the affluence of St. Moritz, Switzerland made us look like fish out of water. While we were not the only black athletes in the Games, we were the only all-black team. We ignored the constraints that society put on us and the way it wanted to view us. As I have mentioned before, we chose to see ourselves not just as Jamaicans trying to bobsled, but as athletes with the talent and the ability to become world class bobsledders.

Looking back, I understand why people would look at us suspiciously and wonder if we were merely a media stunt. I suppose I might have had similar reaction if a group of Germans or Swiss guys who, after only a few months of practice, turned up to go against the powerful West Indian cricket team. It would have been laughable. Therein lies the irony of being a Jamaican bobsledder, particularly one from the original team. It is an irony that has even wider implications. Nothing about our background, society, race or otherwise demands that our opportunities should be limited to certain spheres. Society strongly suggests it. Society suggests that you can't have a Jamaican bobsledder any more than you can have a Swiss cricketer. Of course, we know that it is up to each of us to develop how wide our sphere will be. That is why you can have Barak Obama, an African-American holding the most powerful office in the world; or Ellen Johnson-Sirleaf, a Harvard-educated woman, becoming the first female leader of Liberia; or Stephen Hawking, a man permanently confined to a wheelchair with Lou Gehrig's disease and required to use a speech synthesizer to talk, regarded by his peers as the world's foremost living theoretical physicist.

Debi Thomas also competed in Calgary. She was locked in a rivalry with the East German Katerina Witt in what the media dubbed the "Battle of the Carmens." She became the first African-American to win a Winter Olympic Medal when she finished third behind Katerina and Elizabeth Manley of Canada. Her accomplishment was even more significant to her because many people told her that she could not attend college full-time and still do what she did. She proved them wrong. Shani Davis also had to see himself in a different light in order to become the first black skater to make a U.S. Olympic team when he qualified for the Salt Lake City Games in 2002. He is the first black skater to win a world all-around title, a world sprint title, and the first to win an Olympic Gold medal in an individual event when he captured gold in the 1,000m event in Torino, Italy in 2006. Growing up, Shani had to push against the stereotypical views. As a child in Chicago, he got teased by his friends who could not understand why he would idolize white speed skating champion Bonnie Blair over basketball icon Michael Jordan. Even his dad told him that speed skating was not a sport for black kids. Asked about his accomplishment shortly after his historic win in Torino, Davis commented, "To me, it doesn't matter what color I am." He continued, "Black or white, Asian or Hispanic, it doesn't matter to me as long as the message I'm portraying to people that watch me on TV is positive." The challenges one faces in competing at the Olympics has everything to do with the enormity of the task and nothing to do with how you may be perceived as different.

Sharing a meal with Jeff Woodard (left, USA) and Anders Intlers (deceased, Latvia). La Plagne, 1991.

CHAPTER 30

Equal Opportunity Requires Personal Responsibility

"The price of greatness is responsibility."
Winston Churchill - British Prime Minister

The business world is changing for the better as companies continue to discover the value of having a diverse workforce. It is now much more common than, say, in the 1950's to find a workplace where employees are respected as individuals and are valued for their contributions in accomplishing the mission. At the same time, more and more organizations are fostering an inclusive, supportive, open, challenging and innovative work environment to enable employees to be positive, creative, and reach their full potential. This is essential for the success of any business, especially as we operate more and more in a global economy, and technological advances continue to shrink the size of the world. As in the Olympic Games, individuals from all kinds of backgrounds are being given an equal opportunity to succeed. Of course, equal opportunity does not guarantee equal results. The results you earn are always a consequence of your ability to take advantage of the opportunities you have been afforded.

At some point in our lives, each of us have been unfairly labeled and placed in a box constructed by someone who made certain assumptions about us. But you always have a choice. As the marketplace continues to evolve, you can choose to dwell on such injustices and allow your future prospects to be defined by them, or you can unshackle yourself from them. Being filled with rancor about injustices committed against you will cause you to be let go from your job or your customer base. Your inability to let go of the past will result in you missing a business opportunity or a path that would have otherwise opened up to you. In order to be successful in a competitive environment, you have to move past the stereotypes and the labels, unchain yourself from your perceived limitations and break out of the box. By transcending those barriers and adopting an empowering attitude, societal norms, assumptions, and associations no longer become a consideration or a stumbling block, and you find yourself liberated and able to pursue any goal you can dream of **AND** in the process transform yourself into an invaluable and highly sought after commodity in the business world.

Abebe Bikila was born in the mountains of Ethiopia, the son of a shepherd. When he was old enough, he became a private in the army of Haile Selassie, the emperor of Ethiopia. As part of his military training, he was sent to a camp which was set up by the government after World War II. While there he caught the eye of Onni Niskanen, a Finnish-born Swede who was hired by the Ethiopian government to train potential athletes. When he reported for the start of the marathon in the 1960 Rome Olympics, Abebe Bikila probably would have gone totally unnoticed except for the fact that he was not wearing shoes. By the end of the race he was known as the "Ethiopian who conquered Rome." He broke the World and Olympic marathon records and became the first black African to win an Olympic medal. Without the knowledge and expertise of Niskanen, Bikila would probably still be running in the mountains of Ethiopia. He combined all the information that his coach provided with his exceptional talent for running to become an Olympic Champion. The same approach is also applicable to us today.

You have to take the information that is available in the marketplace and make it relevant to your life and, in so doing, expand your horizons and grow as a person to meet the demands of an ever-changing world. Diversity is about you, as an individual, broadening your outlook. The bottom line is that you have to accept your own uniqueness and embrace your own potential for greatness before others can embrace the differences in you and you in them.

Taking personal responsibility means it is up to **YOU**. You have more control than you believe you do, and when you take over the reins for your personal growth and development not only do you rise above the fray to enjoy personal success and contribute to the success of the team, you are also able to influence and inspire others to pursue their dreams as well. Your success must never be dependent on what your company or the government does. It is not relying on the company to implement some kind of training program that you can sign up for or hoping that affirmative action (although it has its place) or some other piece of legislation will open doors for you. You have to be prepared to open the doors for yourself or, where necessary, kick them in.

There was a time when, not so long ago, sports did not offer the best talent and the stiffest competition it could. Even when minorities were allowed to compete, their performance was always seen through the prism of their ethnicity. Jim Thorpe, the great Native American athlete, won Olympic gold medals in the pentathlon and decathlon. I am in awe of his athletic abilities. His Olympic record in the decathlon stood for nearly two decades. He also played football at the collegiate and professional levels, as well as professional baseball and basketball. Such amazing accomplishments led to the Associated Press naming him the greatest athlete of the first half of the Twentieth Century in 1950. His accomplishments were also described in a racial context. For example, articles about him in the *New York Times* ran the headline, "Indian Thorpe in Olympiad," and, "Redskin from Carlisle Will Strive for Place on American Team." He was stripped of his Olympic Medals because he played baseball for $2 a game, and although the International Olympic Committee restored them in 1983, many felt they were taken away because of his ethnicity.

Systemic racism ensured that blacks and whites could not play in the same professional leagues. In 1920, Fritz Pollard and Bobby Marshall became the first black players in what is now known as the National Football league. But by 1934 there were no black players in the League, reportedly because one of the owners, George Preston Marshall, refused to sign black players and pressured the rest of the League to do the same. When blacks were eventually signed after WWII, they were treated poorly, given lower contracts than their white counterparts and confined to "speed" positions such as defensive backs but excluded from "intelligent" positions such as quarterback and center.

Willie O'Ree became the National Hockey League's version of Jackie Robinson when he debuted with the Boston Bruins in 1958. Sadly, many saw his skin color instead of his hockey skills, and the spectators would often assault him with comments such as, "Go back to the south!" and "How come you're not picking cotton?"

Of course, this is not the case today, and teams compete fiercely to sign the best player available in the market no matter where in the world they might be from. There are several successful black quarterbacks and centers in the NFL, and the NHL has actively promoted diversity throughout the League.

To thrive in an increasingly competitive business environment, companies must make it a priority to create the type of atmosphere that will attract the best new talent, and make it possible for employees to make their fullest contribution. Systemic racism in the past may have allowed athletes to reject a teammate because of his ethnicity, but today it is a different matter. Their chief concern is whether or not the athlete can help them win. If you knew that your paycheck, bonus, medical insurance or some other benefit were dependent to some extent upon the person about to be hired to fill a critical slot, and you were part of the team responsible for selecting this person, what would you really care about?

Wouldn't you want to be able to select from as wide a pool of the best and the brightest you have access to? You wouldn't want a person who shared your ethnic background or religious views if they couldn't do the work, would you? Would you want someone who is not motivated and feels a sense of entitlement because of their social background, or would you prefer to work with someone who, although they looked and sounded totally different from you, had the same work ethic and commitment to excellence as you?

What if you were the person getting hired in this new position? Would you care if you were the only black guy, or woman, or gay person, if your teammates were respecting you as a person and allowing you the autonomy and creative freedom that you need to perform your work? Would it matter to you if your boss's political views were decidedly different from yours? What if the organization allowed you to climb as high as you wanted – would you care if you were the only immigrant, or that you were confined to a wheel chair?

I believe that we will always find subtle differences amongst ourselves that go beyond textbook definitions of diversity, and since we are all imperfect humans, we strive and look for ways to appreciate these differences, to recognize their strengths to the team, or, quite frankly, just ignore them because it has nothing to do with the work at hand. In the final analysis, the only thing that really matters is our results.

The Olympic Movement is built on the philosophy that everyone has a real chance to bring the power of their determination and resolve to pursue their highest aspirations, regardless of race, ethnic background and so on. In fact, the stated goal of the Olympic Movement is to contribute to building a peaceful and better world by educating youth through sport practiced without discrimination of any kind. This is why four guys from a tropical paradise could dare to become Olympic bobsledders, and in the process bring a little flair and color to the sport and the Olympics itself. It is that same philosophy that has allowed Anne Abernathy, affectionately known as "Grandma Luge," a 55-year-old, six-time Olympic luger from the United States Virgin Islands, to compete at the Olympic Games against women who are young enough to be her granddaughters. Likewise, Oscar Pistorius, a double-amputee runner from South Africa. He has also benefited from this philosophy. He was born without the fibula in his lower legs and had his them amputated below the knee at eleven months old. He failed in his bid to compete in the 400m events against able-bodied athletes at the Beijing Olympics. But even he understands that we are given equal opportunity, though not guaranteed equal results.

A few months after I competed in the Calgary Olympics, Jim Abbott took to the mound and pitched a complete game to secure the United States win over Japan in the gold medal game during the XXIV Olympic Games in Seoul, South Korea. It was America's first gold medal in Olympic baseball competition. In high school, Jim was a standout pitcher and quarterback. While at the University of Michigan in 1987, he became the first baseball pitcher to win the James E. Sullivan Award. In 1988 he was voted

Big Ten Athlete of the Year. After his gold medal performance in the 1988 Seoul Olympics, Jim jumped to Major League Baseball where he played for the California Angels, the New York Yankees, the Chicago White Sox, and the Milwaukee Brewers before retiring in 1999. The thing that is most remarkable about Jim Abbott, however, is not his biography, but rather the fact that he had all those accomplishments despite being born without a right hand.

None of the examples I just mentioned, like millions of others pursuing various other interests, are asking for any special arrangements or considerations. The only thing they need is an environment which embraces and respects their differences and simply allows them the opportunity to go for it.

Let's go back to that overhead snapshot of the Olympic Games. What you see is the world coming together as people come together. You see people with similar interests living, working and playing together. That is what it means to live in this new global village. Our new partners may wear different labels; they may be different in their cultural or ethnic background. Your religious or political views may be on opposite sides of the spectrum, but in the end everyone shares the same objectives: to thrive, grow and make a difference.

KEY POINTS TO REMEMBER - LESSON 10

- Neither your race, ethnic background, age or any other arbitrary norm or label can define the limits of your success or prevent you from exploring your full potential.

- Equal opportunity does not guarantee equal results. The results you earn are always a consequence of your ability to take advantage of the opportunities you have been afforded.

- Diversity is about you as an individual broadening your outlook. You have to accept your own uniqueness and embrace your own potential for greatness before others can embrace the differences in us and us in them.

- You have more control over your personal success than you believe you do, but it requires you to take over the reins for your personal growth and development. Your success must never be dependent on what your company or the government does. It is not relying on the company to implement some kind of training program that you can sign up for or hoping that affirmative action or some other piece of legislation will open doors for you. You have to be prepared to open the doors for yourself or, where necessary, kick them in.

ASSIGNMENTS

1. Modify your assumptions about others.
   First seek to understand before being understood.

2. Commit to look past the obvious differences and seek to identify and common ground with others.

3. Learn to recognize how the uniqueness of others adds to the richness of your experiences.

The Keep On Pushing Foundation

The *Keep On Pushing Foundation* is a federally recognized 501(c)3 non-profit organization founded in 2006 by former Jamaican bobsled team captain, Devon Harris. The Foundation was started as a result of Devon's commitment to do whatever it takes to nourish the bodies and minds of the children in his old Kingston neighborhood and elsewhere around the world as he believes these young students have the same potential for success as he did.

Through his Foundation, Devon aims to bring hope to youths in disadvantaged communities around the globe by creating practical opportunities for them to explore their full potential. The *Keep On Pushing Foundation's* initial activities are focused on delivering new computers, books and school supplies as well as a solid breakfast for every elementary school child in Devon's old Waterhouse school district, for, as Devon believes, you cannot learn if you are hungry and lack for the most basic tools to compete in the 21st century.

Since the institution of the breakfast program, the teachers have reported increased attendance as well as improved punctuality, behavior and test scores. Supplementing the breakfast program is a school supplies program where the students are provided with book bags, notebooks and other supplies necessary to support their education.

The Foundation intends to establish computer labs in the schools. These labs will not only serve the students attending the schools but also provide computer training for the 18-23 year-old young adults in the adjacent communities. The Foundation's ultimate goal is to empower these students and young adults to make a better life for themselves.

The Foundation is currently in the early stages of an ambitious plan to build a prototype standalone state of the art kitchen/bakery and dining structure at the Drews Avenue Primary school which Devon attended. The goal is to feed the children as well as use the facility as a source of employment and training for members of the community.

To date, we are pleased that great companies including Charles Schwab, FedEx, Office Depot, Roche, and Ritz-Carlton Golf & Spa Resort in Rose Hall, Jamaica, and organizations such as Mt. Zion Baptist Church in Pleasantville, NJ, Temple Sinai in Cinnaminson, NJ, and George Washington Elementary School, in Mohegan Lake, NY, among others, have supported the *Keep On Pushing Foundation* with in-kind and cash donations.

For more information or to learn how you can support the Foundation activities please visit: **www.keeponpushing.org.**

Bibliography

Anthony, Robert. *Beyond Positive Thinking: A No-Nonsense Formula for Getting the Results You Want.* Newport News, VA: Morgan James, 2004.

Collins, James C. *Good to Great.* New York: HarperBusiness, 2001.

Gawain, Shakti. *Creative Visualization.* Mill Valley, CA: Whatever, 1978.

Givens, Charles. *Superself: Doubling Your Personal Effectiveness.* New York: Simon & Schuster, 1993.

Graham, Stedman. *Diversity: Leaders Not Labels: A New Plan for the 21st Century,* New York: Free Press, 2006.

Maltz, Maxwell. *Psychocybernetics: A New Way to Get More Living Out of Your Life.* Englewood Cliffs, NJ: Prentice-Hall, Inc., 1960.

Newberry, Tommy. *Success Is Not an Accident: Change Your Choices, Change Your Life.* Decatur, GA :Looking Glass Books, 2000.

Rohn, Jim. *The Seasons of Life.* South Lake, TX: Jim Rohn International, 2002.

Staples, Walter. *Think Like a Winner.* Gretna, LA: Pelican Publishing, 1991.

(continued on page 268)

Bibliography (cont.)

Stolz, Paul G. *Adversity Quotient: Turning Obstacles Into Opportunities.* New York: John Wiley and Sons, Inc., 1997.

Tracy, Brian. *Maximum Achievement: Strategies and Skills that will Unlock Your Hidden Powers to Succeed.* New York: Simon & Schuster, 1993.

Van Fleet, James K. *Hidden Power: How to Unleash the Power of Your Subconscious Mind.* Paramus, NJ: Prentice-Hall, 1987.

Index

"f" refers to photograph